DECORATING WITH

COLOR

DECORATING WITH
COLOR

THE BEST OF MARTHA STEWART LIVING

CONTENTS

introduction 6

honeycomb 28

ironstone 10

lustreware 40

delft 20

melon 50

spice 60

celadon 92

sea glass 72

dove 102

jonquil 82

conch shell 112

swatch guide 124

sources 136

credits 141 | index 142

acknowledgments 144

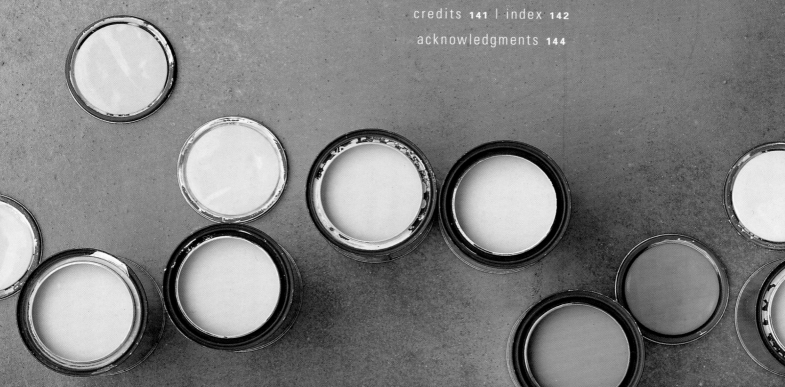

introduction

For most people, the hardest part of decorating is committing to color. Once the paint is on the wall or the fabric has covered the sofa, important decisions have been made that are expensive and time-consuming to revoke. Fearing that they will make a mistake, many people freeze—and put off making a decorating plan. All too often, the result is a home that fills up haphazardly with objects acquired regardless of how their colors harmonize, or don't. But choosing colors and developing designs that work for your home can be fun. With this book, and the palettes and projects described on the following pages, we at MARTHA STEWART LIVING hope to show you how to create rooms that you will find appealing, distinctive, and comfortable.

There are many different ways to use color. Some people are drawn to bold, saturated colors, and they use them freely, painting the hallway fire-engine red, the living room peacock blue, and the kitchen shocking pink. Others fill their spaces with stripes and geometrics and florals. Our approach is very different. The colors used in this book, collected from the pages of MARTHA STEWART LIVING, are a direct result of our sensibility and of our instinct for what makes a room beautiful and inviting.

By and large, the rooms we love are monochromatic, their palettes based on just one main color used throughout. To add interest, we often use three or four shades of the same color, and if we use a second color, it is likely to be a neighboring one on the color wheel (opposite), and thus inherently similar. Because we combine colors that are nearly alike—yellow greens and blue greens, for instance—the rooms speak softly. Most of the eleven palettes in this book were inspired by a beautifully crafted object, like a piece of celadon pottery, or by something glorious from nature, such as a conch shell. None of these objects is truly a single color; looked at from different angles, in varying lights, each turns out to be many shades of one color or two or three.

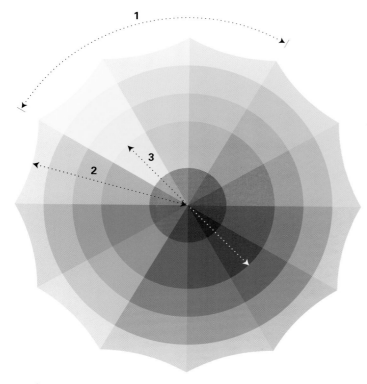

A color wheel lets you look at the primary (red, yellow, and blue) and secondary (orange, purple, and green) colors all at once to see how they relate.

1. NEIGHBORING COLORS
In close proximity on the color wheel, these colors—such as yellow, orange, and peach—mix without clashing, especially in their subtlest tones.

2. MONOCHROMATIC COLOR
Various tones of one color, from light to dark, can be combined to create a rich palette.

3. COMPLEMENTARY COLORS
Every color has an opposite, or complementary, color. Using one of these paired colors (in this case, yellow) along with its complement (purple) will make both colors look more vibrant.

Our taste has been consistent from the beginning. We never employ six or seven colors in a room, because the outcome strikes us as chaotic. If you want to make a bold color statement, do it with an accessory that introduces a colorful accent. A decorator wanting to liven up a room might throw in a teal or orange pillow; we would more likely use black as punctuation, without adding a color. You'll see over and over how we use black paint or dark wood to anchor a room. But if you really want another color, it is often best to pick one from the opposite side of the color wheel. Purple, for instance, in small doses will complement yellow. And

you can use the accent color to create a secondary palette, adding several variations of that shade throughout the room.

At MARTHA STEWART LIVING, we decorate with all colors but never in loud or overdone manifestations. We like every color, from moss green to tomato red, as long as it is not jumbled with too many others. Our favorites were inspired by the natural world, from the eggs of Araucana chickens to the fur of chow chows to the wondrous shells of the sea. Our response might be to pick up a bit of moss from a tree trunk outside a house, for example, and decide to use its soft color somewhere in the living room.

Since we choose colors that are so quiet and so similar, we treat texture the way that others might use pattern or bold color. Damask, which is a variation on a single color, provides complexity, as do materials such as sisal and nubby fabrics. The overall effect is neither monotonous nor faint, in part because no room exists in isolation from its use. By the time you add books, and platters of food, and flowers, and, of course, people and pets, there is plenty going on to engage the eye.

Often, the most difficult step is simply getting started and making some initial choices from the overwhelming array of colors in the world. If there is one lesson to take away from this book, it is this: Find the colors you like, and do not be afraid to use them—one at a time. For instance, if you like orange and you want to paint your walls a pale apricot, do not feel you have to choose a contrasting color, like brown, for the trim. Paint the trim a different shade of apricot, and the end result will be calm rather than busy. In essence, if we don't like a color enough to see it all over a room, we don't want to see it at all.

How, then, do you know what you like? The key is to pay attention to yourself and what you respond to instead of listening to your friends' dos and don'ts or to decorators' forecasts of tomorrow's hot color trends. Start, perhaps, by going into your living room and looking around. What single item do you most love and enjoy? If you had to give up all but one possession in that room, what would you keep? Then take a careful look at your chosen object. There is a good chance that its color speaks to you emotionally, making you feel happy and comforted. Go with that instinct, at least as a starting point.

Or go to the paint store. Look at all the paint chips, and simply let yourself react. Do that over and over, and see whether you keep returning to the same colors or the same family of colors.

ABOVE At Martha's television-studio office, nearly every surface has been painted in one of her favorite colors, jadeite green. The wooden table on castors, the vintage office furniture, and the standard-issue file cabinets are all sprayed in auto-body paint to achieve a smooth finish. The office chair and stool are upholstered in matching leather; even the vintage letter tray is painted in jadeite.

When it is clear that you are drawn to certain tones, visit a fabric store and note where your eye takes you. At home, look in your closets and cupboards at the choices you have made over time. Above all, don't expect to arrive at a palette in five or ten minutes. Collect the paint chips and fabric swatches that appeal to you, without thinking about which material will go on which chair. If you buy each material in isolation, you will find it difficult to achieve the look you want; but if you collect six or seven variations on your favorite colors and textures, then you can begin to assign them to the wall or the sofa or the woodwork. You will see in each chapter of this book how we combine swatches of fabric and other materials to begin mapping out a particular room's decor.

While you are trying to figure out which colors you like, look through the palettes we have included here. Each chapter is about a family of colors rather than a single color. We begin with the object that inspired the colors in a palette and then show how that palette translates into fabrics, paints, and wall coverings. In the photographs, you will see the same color manifested differently in various settings, in tones both gentle and strong, sometimes combined with another color, in environments contemporary and traditional. We have also included a section called "Swatch Guide," which contains even more ideas and materials for each family of colors. Most likely, you'll feel powerfully drawn to one or two or three. There's a chance that some of them will leave you cold. Go with those reactions and learn from them.

Once you have some colors, the best approach is to start slowly. Always paint large test patches on several different walls, so you can see the effect in a variety of lights. You'll want to view a few

shades of a color at different times of day and at night. The view through your windows also makes a difference: In certain lights, for instance, yellow paint on a kitchen wall will look green if there are trees directly outside.

If you are partial to a number of palettes, think about how they might work together. For example, if you choose sea glass for your living room and melon for your kitchen, you might want to create a transitional space—in the connecting hallway, perhaps—that ties those rooms together. Or if you adore a color such as pumpkin but do not want it on a wall or furniture, use it inside a cabinet or closet, so you can still enjoy the color without having to work your entire palette around it.

Every surface of your home presents an opportunity to play with color. Place a bouquet of pink flowers on a dresser, and the entire room changes. Likewise, you can create two very different effects in a gray dining room by setting the table with either green or red-and-white plates. And don't forget that, in most cases,

it makes sense not to leave the ceiling white. That surface presents another chance to use color and to manipulate light. Consider covering it with a lighter shade of your wall color. Just don't make the ceiling a darker color; it will feel as if it is falling in.

Surround yourself with colors that please you, and your home will feel like a true representation of you. Above all, it will be a more comfortable place, one that soothes and shelters.

Passionate defenders of white do not consider it to be lacking in color; they see it instead as an amalgam of all colors, containing every shade and shadow in the world. The subtlety of white, for those who choose to perceive it, is endlessly satisfying. And in few objects is its charm more apparent than in ironstone, the modest white-glazed ceramic

IRONSTONE

originally produced in England. As ironstone ages, the color softens and loses its sharpness, tending toward brown or yellow. Although it is now avidly collected and can be expensive, ironstone began as an affordable alternative to easily chipped china, and was meant primarily for everyday dinners or simple meals in the kitchen. British manufacturers often applied colorful patterns to the dishes sold at home, but much of the ironstone shipped to the United States had only the plain white glaze, appealing to the desire for hygienic materials. Whether that is still a factor in its popularity, there is no question that ironstone makes a lovely accompaniment to any occasion.

The variations in ironstone produce whites with undertones of blue, gray, yellow, and pink, a palette that can be surprisingly complex when combined with different textures. Close study usually reveals that a warm white tends toward yellow or pink and a cool one toward blue or gray. In general, it is easier to combine warm whites with other warm colors and cool whites with cool colors. Because of their undertones of color, off-whites are more forgiving than stark whites on uneven walls or worn woodwork.

SWATCHES Just because a room is decorated in various shades of pure white, off-white, and gray does not mean that it is simple to put together. It is important to collect all of the fabrics and paints that you are thinking of using and put them side by side to make sure that their underlying tones combine well. The fabrics and paints used here complement one another, and they are enlivened by several sparkling elements. The chandelier and the gilt mirror frame, represented in the swatch packet by the piece of crystal and the ribbon, respectively, reflect light.

OPPOSITE This dining room's simple, pale floor is created by painting shades of white, gray, and cream in a diamond pattern, providing graphic interest without using loud colors. In the middle of the table, graniteware (actually tin enameled to look like granite) repeats the gray of the floor. In such a monochromatic space, it is easy and fun to introduce a color unrelated to the palette, such as the two red chairs.

There is no such thing as a single shade of ironstone, unaffected by its environment. Likewise, the nature of the light striking white paint changes its color. **RIGHT, FROM TOP** The wall looks pale and bleached in northern, indirect light, which diminishes the contrast between the wall and the trim; the white chair and flowers blend seamlessly with the other whites around them. Later in the day, the sun's rays wash the same wall in yellow. At night, incandescent light draws out peach and yellow around the sconce, while the rest of the wall becomes a moody bluish gray. **ABOVE** Creamy walls establish a sense of warmth and comfort, while bright white trim brings crispness and definition. **OPPOSITE** In a nearly all-white room, other colors, such as the yellow of the tablecloth—and the black of the dog, of course—can make a big statement. The white is particularly radiant in front of the lush green garden.

Two all-white rooms take opposite tacks, one relying on cool whites and the other on warm. **ABOVE** In this room, only the candles are chalk white. The sofa is upholstered in shades of silvery taupe and beige, and on the wall, crystal sconces and a silver frame further enhance the gleam. **OPPOSITE** On the shelf of a mirrored mantelpiece, reflective mercury-glass lamps, vases, and other vessels provide a warm, luminous setting for the roses that bring the only touch of intense color.

projects

DOT CUTOUTS

Simple holes become sophisticated ornaments when they are clustered in geometric patterns. The decorative cutouts on this wastebasket and stool were created with an electric drill.

1. First, design a pattern. Dot patterns can be inspired by those around you, such as mosaic-tile configurations, tea strainers, or telephone mouthpieces. Before putting drill bit to wood, experiment on paper, using adhesive dots or a hole punch to work out a pattern that suits the dimensions of the object to be drilled. Or on a photocopier, simply enlarge the template shown below to make our wastebasket design. **2.** It's worth taking time to build your confidence with a drill by practicing on scrap lumber. **3.** Standard auger bits and bits of the four types shown here can make all of the holes in this project, as well as others that you may want to devise. Depending on how far you press its tapered tip into a piece of wood, a single countersink bit can bore cone-shaped indentations in a variety of sizes—the harder you press, the wider and deeper the hollow. The central spike of a brad-point bit makes it easy to align the drill with the center of the hole to be drilled. Forstner bits carve larger holes into thicker woods. A hole-saw attachment is the best for making doorknob-size holes. Just a slight change of bit size can enhance the decorative effect of a cutout pattern. The stylized flowers and snowflake on this wastebasket and stool were accomplished using only three bit sizes: ¼-inch, 5/16-inch, and 7/16-inch. Keep bits sharp by using them only on the materials indicated by the manufacturer, and clean with a soft cloth after use. **4.** After sanding and priming the surface that is to be drilled, place it on a stable base, such as sawhorses or a workbench, where you can operate the drill at a comfortable working height. If possible, set up a precision drill guide, a metal stand that holds the drill and bit perpendicular to the surface. As drill bits tend to enter wood more cleanly than they leave it, clamp a second board (preferably a piece of scrap lumber that's at least ½ inch thick) to the backside of the surface being drilled to give the bit something to bite into as it exits the hole, creating a neat edge. Drilling a clean hole through plywood or particle board is almost impossible; solid wood is your best bet. For extra protection against having wood splinter or break, space the holes no less than ⅜ inch apart. Drill using a corded tool (drilling multiple holes may drain the battery of a cordless drill before the job is complete). Apply a coat of paint; file the insides of the holes, and sand all surfaces; finish with a topcoat of paint.

MATERIALS

wastebasket

stool

drill

assorted drill bits

clamp

extra wood

paint

sandpaper

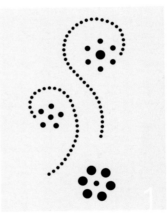

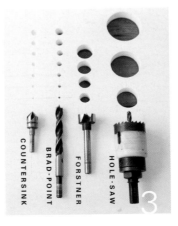

COUNTERSINK   BRAD-POINT   FORSTNER   HOLE-SAW

BEFORE

AFTER

People think of wallpaper as fixed and immutable, and yet it can be transformed when you redecorate a room. With this fading glaze, a strong wallpaper pattern can be muted and its colors softened.

Glazing can be a deliberate part of your wallpapering plan. Keep in mind that some papers, including solid vinyl paper, string cloth, and grass cloth, do not accept glazes well. To make a fading glaze, mix approximately one part latex glazing liquid to one part latex interior white paint. Add enough water to equal ¼ to ½ of the mixture, depending on how thick (opaque) you want the glaze to be. Use flat paint for a fading glaze with a matte finish. For a finish with more sheen, use satin paint. High-gloss paint can cause a fading glaze to yellow, so for a glossy finish, add a high-gloss sealer, such as a waterborne polyurethane, to a mixture with satin paint. When testing a fading glaze, always let the test area dry completely, since the glaze can change as it dries. Mix glazes thoroughly and test before applying to wallpaper; a large remnant of flattened, unused wallpaper is the ideal test surface. Next, inspect the wallpaper on the wall. Make sure the seams are all glued flat in place, then choose an inconspicuous patch of wallpaper to test the glaze again. Choose a spot you feel confident can remain obscured if the paper peels or if some areas soak up too much glaze and others none at all: These results mean glazing is not right for your wallpaper. If the glaze will take to your wallpaper, pat it on with lint-free cotton rags in a tamping or swirling motion. Work in sections, from one side of the wall to the other, applying the glaze so it overlaps slightly with the edge of the wet area just applied. Keep in mind that glaze dries quickly—applying it to areas that have already dried may result in areas of high opacity. For corners or molding, apply glaze with a paintbrush, then pat with a rag to mask the strokes.

MATERIALS

latex glazing liquid

latex white paint

cotton rags

paintbrush

When people are asked to name a favorite color, they often choose blue. It is not surprising. Blue is the color of the sky, and so it surrounds us from the day we are born, like a comforting quilt. As children, we splash in the dark-blue waves of the ocean or in the tropics' aquamarine pools. Maybe it is because sky and water seem to embrace us that blue

DELFT

is so calming. Experiments have shown that gazing at something blue will reduce both blood pressure and heart rate. But this hue is also expansive and seems to go on forever. Although blue jeans have become an emblem of American style, we can stake no national claim to blue, a color that has been popular in every culture since the ability to set dye was established. Internationally beloved are dishes from the Dutch factories in Delft, themselves inspired by the blue-and-white porcelains of China. Delft vividly shows the possibilities in blue, because it is not just one shade but a mélange of many, greater in complexity and sophistication than a single tone.

There are thousands of blues, including the purple blue of hydrangea blossoms, the green blue of a tranquil sea, and the dark gray blue of a stormy sky. In this palette we focus on true blues in shades from light to dark, with gray added in some cases to provide depth. Blue is considered a cool color because it appears to recede, as opposed to a warm color, such as red, which seems to advance. Most blues are even more appealing when juxtaposed with other shades of blue or with white, just as a summer sky is enhanced by bright cumulus clouds.

SWATCHES A spectrum of blues was used in this living room, opposite. The blues of the Delft tiles and transferware plates are dark and almost purple, and the blue of the lamp is a shade of peacock. The rich sky blue that was painted on the wall, shown above in the top color chip, serves to tie the various blues together. Although there are several patterned fabrics used in this room, they are kept from overwhelming the space through a liberal use of white. The wood trim and the coffee table were painted white, and the fabric on the reading chair has a white background.

OPPOSITE This room was inspired by the collection of tiles and plates on the wall. The consistency of their color helps achieve an almost abstract effect, even though several of the individual pieces are filled with pictorial detail. If multiple colors had been used, the assemblage would have looked chaotic. The dark wood of the chair, the picture frame, and the cabinet keeps the room from seeming too soft and delicate.

OPPOSITE This guest room is rich in detail, and yet because only blue, white, and black are used, it still feels soothing. The white latticework on the walls adds interest to a small room that otherwise might feel spartan. Because the blue chair blends into the wall, it doesn't take up much visual space, keeping the room from feeling cramped. The solid black of the lampshade and picture frame helps ground the dreaminess of the sky blue. **ABOVE LEFT** Although white provides the freshest, cleanest foundation for a bathroom, it is pleasing to inject some color. Here, the medicine cabinet was refitted with a new back of blue-tinted mirror. Because blue is a color that recedes, it makes the cabinet appear deeper, its interior almost watery. **ABOVE RIGHT** Primarily gray, black, and white, this bedroom gets a dramatic streak of color from a sapphire duvet cover. Even someone who finds blue vapid in its softer shades might reconsider its potential after seeing how it is used here.

ABOVE The slanted ceiling in this garret guest room was painted blue to make the room feel more spacious. But that airiness needs a counterpoint, so multihued pillow shams were added. The blue ribbon holding the picture frame enables a small piece of art to fill a large area, provides another strong shot of color, and creates a focal point that brings the room together. A dark spool-turned bed was painted white to avoid competing with the predominant blue.

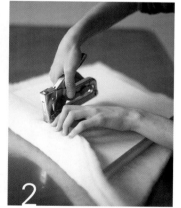

SUN-SILHOUETTE CHAIRS

With the power of the sun, you can make an original and dramatic blue fabric that is at home in both traditional and contemporary environments. The seat cushions of the white chairs at left were recovered with a light-sensitive fabric that had been imprinted with the image of flower stalks. You may also create sun-block fabrics with leaves, shells, or any other graphically distinctive object.

This is a project best saved for a sunny day. The sun's rays react with the fabric, turning exposed areas blue while blocked areas remain white. When ready to use, remove the fabric from the protective black bag it comes in. Working indoors, out of direct sunlight, cut the fabric 4 inches longer than the seat on all sides. With straight pins, pin the fabric, slightly taut, to a piece of cardboard. **1.** Arrange flowers or other objects on the fabric as desired, pinning each securely. Place the fabric in direct sunlight. Without moving it, let sit for the amount of time specified in the fabric's directions. Take indoors immediately, and unpin the objects (there will only be a faint image of the objects at this point). Rinse the fabric under running water, gently agitating, until the water runs clear. Lay it flat in a dark room to dry. With the iron on the coolest set-

MATERIALS

light-sensitive fabric

seat board

cardboard

flowers

iron

pressing cloth

foam

batting fabric

staple gun

upholstery fabric

ting, iron the back of the fabric with a pressing cloth laid over it. To cover the seat, trace the seat board onto 1-inch-thick foam; add ⅛ inch all around, and cut out. Cut cotton batting 4 inches longer than the seat on all sides. Lay the batting flat; center the foam and seat board on top. **2.** Wrap one side of the batting over the seat, and staple 1½ inches from the edge. Wrap the opposite side over, and staple. Repeat on the remaining sides. **3.** Lay the fabric facedown; place the seat on the fabric, cushion side down, and use the same method to attach. To finish, cut the upholstery fabric 1 inch shorter than the seat on all sides; fold and press the edges. Place on underside of seat so that the edges of the upholstery fabric cover the edges of the designed fabric. **4.** Secure with staples at 2-inch intervals. Keep the chairs out of direct sunlight to prevent fading.

Honey is so magical that throughout most of history people believed it dropped from the heavens and was collected by bees. Other theories, of course, were developed to explain its source, but not until the 1700s did people discover that the ambrosia was in fact produced by bees. Like little factories, bees collect nectar from flowers and

HONEYCOMB

turn it into honey, storing it in their honeycombs. In certain lights, honey looks like liquid gold, and in many religions and cultures, its cachet rivals that of the precious metal. In an ancient pagan ritual, the door of a new home was anointed with milk and honey to wish peace and prosperity upon its inhabitants. When Jewish people celebrate the new year, they ritually dip apples into honey to express the hope that the days ahead will be sweet. And though we now have a scientific explanation for honey, it still seems like a divine gift: a glowing river of gold, luxuriously rich on the tongue, providing an evanescent hint of the flower that offered its nectar to industrious bees.

PALE TONES

DARK ACCENTS

BROWN TONES

GREEN TONES

Real honey comes in any number of shades, depending on which flower supplied the nectar that was processed by the bees. Some honeys are a deep, rich brown; others are nearly colorless. Medium shades include pale yellow, amber, and even green. This is a restrained palette rather than one that contains a wide range of shades. Although honey can incline toward green, brown, or pink, there is a goldenness to each shade, an inherent light and warmth that gives the palette its power.

SWATCHES The materials for this room, opposite, were chosen with the intention of creating a quiet, understated space. The shades of the honeycomb palette range from golden to greenish, so it is important to assemble potential fabrics and see how they look together. Otherwise, it can be difficult to determine their underlying tints. Something that looks khaki on its own, for example, may suddenly appear pinkish when it is placed next to another fabric. Once you have a harmonious collection, make sure the colors do not match so closely as to be dull. The fabrics shown above complement one another, but they make up a wide range of neutrals with undertones from yellow to green.

OPPOSITE This dining room relies on a subtle mix of golden-honey beiges. It also takes advantage of an equally subtle collection of shapes, from the svelte white pottery inside the Swedish armoire to the cross-backed dining chairs to the chunky wood table base. The sofa has a curvaceous wood frame, and the stained floor, gently worn from use, has the patina of a well-loved antique.

ABOVE The parlor at Turkey Hill is decorated monochromatically, with a few pieces of dark wood furniture providing anchorage. It is visually engaging because of a wealth of textures, including the sofa's damask cover, the crystals on the chandelier, the wooden slats in the blinds, and the gilt on the mirror. In fact, no single object is solely one color. Even the floor is stenciled to provide quiet contrast, and the drabware displayed on the walls is highlighted in gold.

RIGHT This Venetian-glass chandelier is an unexpected luxury in a summer retreat, but its light-hearted flamboyance inspired a corner of the living room at Martha's East Hampton home. The glazed, shiny linen on the chairs complements the chandelier's color. Even though they are substantial pieces of furniture, the chairs seem to melt away, while the light plays on the floor around them. **BELOW** The glass panels of this old cabinet were backed with vintage fabric to hide the dishes within while also creating a lovely point of interest. Hanging on the wall above is a pair of drabware plates with a pinkish cast that goes well with the red and gold fabric. Objects of disparate shapes, such as the pitchers arranged on top of the cabinet, make a handsome cluster when they are in the same color range. If they were all different colors, the same combination might look like a hodgepodge. The reddish brown velvet on the chair makes use of the same red undertone as the collection of pitchers.

ABOVE In this corner of the Turkey Hill kitchen, one of Martha's chows, Paw Paw, fits right into the honey palette. This is a room defined by subtle detail and light-reflecting objects. Gilded pressed tin attached to the window shade transforms it, heightening the impact of simple curtains made from painter's canvas. The etched sconces and the brick floor also add texture. **OPPOSITE** The palette in this room was inspired by a chalk-striped wool quilt with silk lining and old buttons. Honey combines particularly well with gray. Here, that pairing plays out in the pillowcases and on the headboard, creating a guest bedroom with universal appeal.

LEFT The rich honey color on these walls and on the ceiling highlights details, such as the images of black Scotties in black frames and the white trim. When only one color from the palette is used, the room will be more striking if the shade is somewhat dark, as it is here. The ceiling is a bit lighter but still the same hue. The wood floor is reddish, providing a nice contrast to the green undertones of the sea-grass rug. **BELOW** This modern dining room could seem austere, but the warmth inherent in the honey-colored wood keeps the spare lines from feeling chilly. The lampshades are made from thin wood veneer that looks even more golden when illuminated from within.

ANTIQUING A CHAIR

This Sheraton-style side chair, left, was transformed in a few hours. Though once unremarkable in a dark-mahogany stain, bottom left, it now wears the charming signs of age—paint worn away on the chair back and the fronts of the legs, recesses tinged with darkness.

Antiquing with paint is one of the simplest—and most satisfying—ways to dress up a drab wooden chair and redefine your decor. In just a few hours, you can give a plain piece a rich, beautiful patina that looks as if it took years to develop. Two compatible colors of paint are applied, one over the other. The top layer is then distressed, using warm water and steel wool. The object is to make the paint look as though it has worn away over years of use: Concentrate on areas that get regular contact—the fronts of the legs, the edges and top of the chair back. Don't remove too much paint at once; you want the piece to look aged, not abused. A layer of tinted paste wax is applied to the chair, then buffed. This step seals the surface and gives a hazy, mellow finish; it also imitates the darkened appearance that furniture develops over time. Nearly any piece of wood furniture is a good candidate for antiquing. Visit tag sales and flea markets, and look in your attic—you might already have the perfect piece. Under no circumstances should you paint over a genuine antique. An untouched vintage Windsor chair, for example, can be worth thousands of dollars. Look for plain wood pieces that are strong and functional but not treasures in themselves. Chairs mass-produced in the 1950s, made from sturdy but inexpensive materials, are ideal choices. Look for pieces that aren't fussy but have some recessed embellishment—the tinted wax needs a place to settle, or the effect won't be as evident. The easiest chairs to work with have removable seats. Take these off before you begin working. If the seat is not removable, wrap the upholstery in plastic, sealing it with masking tape.

MATERIALS

1. 200-grit sandpaper
2. masking tape and painter's gloves
3. water-based primer
4. two coordinating colors of latex paint
5. paintbrushes
6. artist's palette, clear paste wax, spackling knife, cotton cloth
7. artist's oil paints
8. rottenstone (optional)
9. coarse steel wool

TECHNIQUE When choosing colors, let the existing decor in a room inspire you. Select two paints that are similar in hue, one lighter than the other, and test them on scraps of wood. Experiment with a lighter undercoat and a darker topcoat, and vice versa. The effect is especially nice when the accent looks like a worn or faded version of the dominant color. Above all, in each step of the process, use a gentle approach: It's much easier to create signs of age than to erase them. If you're working with a previously painted chair, clean the surface with a soft, damp cloth, fill in any holes with wood filler, and lightly sand. New, plain wood should also be lightly sanded. **1.** Using a natural-bristle brush, apply a water-based primer. For painted wood, be sure to use a primer specifically made to stick to a painted surface. Bare wood may require several coats of primer to fill in the grain and to build up a smooth surface. **2.** After the primer has dried completely, apply a coat of the accent-color latex paint, using a nylon-polyester paintbrush. Apply paint heavily, but avoid drips. Use the sides of the brush to create ridges in the paint; once the paint begins to dry, drag the brush through it to accentuate the texture even more. You may need two coats to cover the chair well. Let dry thoroughly, at least six hours. **3.** Apply the dominant color. Cover the chair completely, but in a thinner layer than the undercoat. Set aside until the paint is dry to the touch—about one hour— but not completely dry. **4.** Distress the topcoat, allowing some of the accent color to show through: Working in small sections, about one square foot at a time, rub the chair with a damp rag, then lightly rub the surface with steel wool, wearing away some of the paint. Apply more pressure for a more distressed appearance. Overlap sections slightly to avoid delineating lines. Finish by lightly sanding with fine sandpaper. **5.** On an artist's palette, combine clear paste wax with a small amount of artist's oil paint and rottenstone, if using, and mix well with a spackling knife. Rottenstone will make the wax heavier and darker, providing a more antiqued look. Begin with a light hand—you can always add more color later, but removing wax that is too dark is more difficult. If you do end up with too dark a color, use mineral spirits to remove the wax, and start over. **6.** Apply a light layer of wax to the chair with a soft, clean cloth. Work the wax into the recesses, taking care not to miss any spots. If an area is hard to reach, use a bristle brush. Allow the wax to dry fifteen minutes, then check the color; if it isn't dark enough, apply the tinted wax again. **7.** Once you're satisfied with the color and the wax has dried, use a soft cotton cloth rolled into a ball to buff the chair. This will remove excess wax from the flat surfaces but not from the recessed areas. **8.** The finished chair mimics the patina of age: The paint is worn but not battered, and the grooved areas are darkened.

Anyone encountering lustreware for the first time is in for a treat. This charming pottery comes in a variety of tints and iridescent glazes that glint in the light like polished metal. Even though these antiques look fancy, they are not expensive. Because lustreware was a widely manufactured item in nineteenth-century England, it remains affordable today.

LUSTRE-WARE

The rich spectrum of colors helps define lustreware. A platinum glaze made some pieces resemble silver. Copper lustre was created with a glaze that in fact used gold, laid over a red-clay base; some of the most appealing copper lustreware has touches of blue and gold. Pink lustre was made by applying a gold lustre over a white base. The types of pieces—from teacups to coffeepots to milk jugs—differ as much as the colors. Some lustreware is adorned with primitively drawn scenes, while other examples have simple abstract or floral patterns. All are naive versions of finer wares, comfortable and unintimidating, approachable and yet out of the ordinary.

The colors in the lustreware palette mimic those of the pottery, from pale pinkish purples and plums to deeper blue violets. Used most easily with white, the palette becomes richer and more sophisticated when set against warm or cool grays. Its own warm tones work especially well with deep reddish browns, and each color benefits from a bit of sparkle. To achieve lustreware's iridescence, use several shades of color and then add accents of silver, gold, or another reflective finish.

SWATCHES These paints and fabrics present the silver side of the palette, used throughout the room opposite, from the purple-gray walls to the shimmery curtains. Touches of mirror and mercury glass in the curtain tie-back and in the valance holders reflect the light. The room is also a study in opposites: dark wood played against white paint, shiny fabrics next to matte walls, plain materials mixed with fancy ones. The modest sisal rug contrasts with the rich elegance of the silk damask and duchess-satin curtains. Just as juxtaposing the humble and the elaborate adds interest, so too does combining smooth and textured surfaces when you would rather not use patterned fabrics or rugs.

OPPOSITE Both pale and saturated shades of the lustreware palette were put to use in this living room, as shown in the sofa cushion and the wall paint, respectively. Yet the white trim paint and the upholstery of the sofa frame keep the overall look restrained. The brown wood of the furniture and floor provides another element of contrast. On the table sits a lustreware pitcher and a bouquet of anemones. The Early American faceted mirrored sconce shows how great an impact even a small reflective object can have on a room.

OPPOSITE Deep, rich colors on the walls, floor, and furniture offer a daringly intense version of the lustreware palette. With only a trace of white in the entire room, this decor relies on the reflective quality of materials to add brightness. Dark matte walls are relieved by lustrous satins and the gleam of a modern standing lamp. **LEFT** A coat of pale blue lavender paint makes a hospital bed more inviting. Its clean lines and hard material contrast with the sinuous contours of the woven wicker chair and table. The three colors used on the stacked bed pillows are pulled directly from colors in the antique quilt. **ABOVE** This room embodies a lighter application of the palette. The same blues and browns appear as in the room at left, but here much more white mediates between them. Warm, coppery red browns in the table and chair and on the floor are played against purple-blue walls. Although the architecture here is traditional, the space ultimately feels more contemporary because of its bold geometric floor pattern and the spare use of furniture and other objects.

ABOVE This old-fashioned bedroom combines several tones of the palette with white to create a restful setting. The ornate wicker-paneled beds are painted white, as is the bedside table, to keep the room looking crisp and uncluttered. The satin pillows evoke not only the color of lustreware but also its luminosity. **LEFT** This is an utterly modern room that incorporates a similar color scheme and several reflective elements—including the mirror on the wall, the lamp and clock on the bedside table, and the linens on the bed. Three colors from the palette cover the pillows, and top sheets with a barely detectable sheen were used to make the duvet cover. **OPPOSITE** A lustreware tray and collection of saucers compose a graphic arrangement when they are hung against a medium-tone silvery-gray wall. Silver candlesticks placed against the same background create a gray-on-gray effect.

BELOW Here, a wall in purple gray, one of the deepest tones of the lustreware palette, emphasizes the contours of white pillars used as candle stands. When rooms have attractive moldings or other interesting architectural details, they will receive the attention they deserve when painted white to contrast with dark walls. Dishes hung symmetrically on either side of the doorway serve as both decoration and candle reflectors.

HIDDEN SPACES

Style need not always be expressed on a grand scale. It is easy to lend personality and charm to small spaces with a change of color. Paint the inside of a closet or cabinet in an unexpected shade, or line a drawer with pretty paper or fabric.

It may seem pointless to take trouble over a space that few people will see, but with minimal effort you will not only rescue a nook or cranny from obscurity but also reward yourself with a dose of color every time you open the drawer or the door. You may also make the space within work more efficiently. After all, it is hard to decorate any part of the house—especially a hideaway—without organizing it first. Above, lavender and mauve-tinted lustreware, transferware, and glass inspired the purple-painted interior of an off-white cabinet. Reflections from the glossy paint bathe every object on the shelves in soft color. At right, the drawer of a dark, dignified antique table opens to reveal a sprightly tone and pattern. Italian floral-print paper lines the drawer itself, as well as two removable balsa trays. Bought at a crafts store, the new trays were stained to match the old drawer. Paper was cut to fit the drawer bottom and then laid without adhesive to avoid marring the original finish. Inside the balsa trays, however, double-sided tape holds the paper in place.

Judged on their outward appearance, most melons are anything but beautiful. In fact, some are almost unsightly, with rough skin that looks and feels as if it belongs on an alligator. Maybe that is why it is such a delight to cut open a melon and catch the first glimpse of that burst of color: the luscious orange or the bright pink red or the pale green within.

MELON

The cheerful tones of the melon palette remind us of summer—of perfectly rounded bite-size pieces of honeydew luring us to the breakfast table, or thick slices of watermelon eaten at the end of a long day as fireflies flicker in the dusk. Melon is naturally sweet and delicious, with a scent and flavor that can make refined sugar seem dull by comparison. But it is impossible to imagine the taste without the color, more dazzling and yet more subtle than anything most humans could create. When picked at just the right moment and eaten at peak flavor, a melon is among summer's greatest luxuries, a reason to endure the long, hot days so crucial to its ripening.

The melon palette could also be called sherbet because of its intense colors, softened with a bit of cream. It contains more colors than we usually mix, ranging from soft shades of peach and honeydew to the strong grenadine of watermelon. Because they all live on the same side of the color wheel, these colors combine easily. When used together, they are best mixed in their palest tints so as not to feel cacophonous or jarring. The hottest shades, used sparingly, make stunning accents.

HONEYDEW TONES

HOT ACCENTS

PEACHY TONES

SWATCHES Each of the colors in this bedroom, opposite, has a strong yellow undertone. It is more obvious in the green of the walls and the golden hue of the pillowcase, although the warm tones of the faux-bamboo furniture also have a definite yellow cast. The palette is kept light and airy with plenty of white—in the curtains, the bedding, the lampshades, and the painted armchair. And like many of our favorite rooms, this one benefits from touches of black, found here in the early-twentieth-century writing desk and in the Greek key detail on the lamps.

OPPOSITE When used at full intensity, as they are in this bedroom, the colors of the melon palette are much like the fruit itself: lush and crisp and summery. The space is unified by its many neutrals, from the faux-bamboo bed to the sisal rug to the white lampshades and dotted-Swiss curtains. The bright yellow of the pillowcase and the flowers balances the equally strong green of the walls.

Any color in the melon palette can be used by itself to make a strong statement, or it may be applied faintly to a variety of surfaces. It all depends on which color you find most compelling. **OPPOSITE** In this country dining room, gentle colors combine with such neutrals as the white on the walls and the dark wood table. It is the vivid orange-red silk lampshade, reminiscent of watermelon, that turns this space into something far more striking and memorable than it would otherwise be. **ABOVE** This is a very different way to express affection for the palette. Here, melon tones—especially greens—are used on nearly every surface, and yet no single color dominates the room. The effect is understated and cumulative. The accent of purple alliums illustrates the effectiveness of using a tone from the opposite side of the color wheel for punctuation. **RIGHT** Warm candlelight glowing through a variety of pale melon-colored glass containers demonstrates a subtle application of the palette.

This East Hampton bedroom employs every color in the palette, but with gossamer lightness. It also presents an excellent example of how bed linens can determine the palette of an entire room. In this instance, the quilt, a floral tablecloth that has been backed with linen and tufted, serves as the focal point. The white of the matelassé bedspread—exquisitely modulated by its texture—sets off the various shades of melon, especially those of the headboard and the pale watermelon walls.

BELOW The owner of this house in Maine was inspired by the colorful artwork of the children she teaches, as this sunny area clearly shows. The stairway, which was originally surrounded by drab walls and a nearly black banister, was brought to life with an unorthodox shade of peachy melon paint. The walls were painted a paler shade of the trim's color. Orange pine floors complete the color palette.

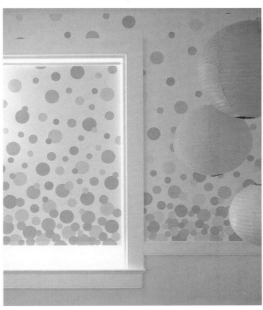

POLKA-DOT STENCILS

Having burst out of their usual grid, polka dots in three sizes and colors pour down the walls of a child's bedroom like a shower of confetti, piling up on the chair rail and fluttering down the blackout shade.

To create this effect—which could be confined to a window shade or a closet door—use circle templates and a utility knife to make nine reusable stencils (three in each of three sizes) from low-tack self-adhesive vinyl. (Sticky vinyl stencils ensure clean, sharp circles.) Attach a stencil to a wall or shade, then paint the section of wall inside the circle with latex paint. When the paint is dry, lift the stencil. Repeat with other colors and stencil sizes, overlapping some of the circles; use one stencil of each size for each paint color. Increase the density of the dots as you work from top to bottom to suggest confetti falling onto a solid surface.

MATERIALS

circle templates

utility knife

self-adhesive vinyl

latex paint

paintbrush

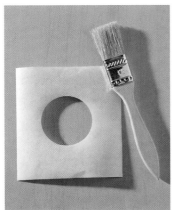

You might not guess, looking at a clove, what potent flavor lies within. But crack it open, and the smell will instantly transport you to another time and place. Spice is something that you understand only as you experience it. And often the best results are achieved by the melding of many. Just as a recipe's success lies in the careful and subtle blending of

SPICE

spices, so, too, do the colors in this palette work best when combined with one another. The darkness of the palette can be intimidating at first, but when you look at how warmly it can fill a space, any apprehension disappears. The colors are as rich and rewarding as some of our favorite spices—star anise, nutmeg, coriander, and cinnamon, among others. We may now take them for granted, but these spices were once rare and costly, and people traveled across the world to obtain them. Today they are much easier to find, but their exotic flavors and colors continue to inspire us, and to enrich our lives as they have enriched others, down through the centuries.

There is no such thing as just a simple brown, and nothing illustrates that better than this palette. Brown isn't a dull color that goes with everything; it is a hue that encompasses tones of many others. There are red browns and green browns, purple browns and gray browns. The spice palette can be unobtrusive or, in its own subtle way, quite rich, ranging from light camel to the blackest burnt umber. In its palest shades, it is an easy neutral. At its darkest, it works well when balanced with white, silver, or gold, all of which keep it upbeat, not somber.

SWATCHES Materials with strong patterns and simple shapes lend a modern edge to a mostly traditional room, opposite. The colors were keyed to those of a favorite fabric, the plaid on the chairs. The tartan's deepest stripes set the tone for the dark walls and folding screen; the camel background inspired the solid camel seats and backs.

The touch of red in the chairs' plaid is reinforced by the red tartan on the footstool and in the solid red throw on top. Gilded borders on the screen panels lighten a dark corner of the room. The burlap–like curtains let light in, yet their texture makes them strong enough to hold their own alongside the other bold fabrics.

OPPOSITE This sitting area at one end of a guest room is warm and comfortable yet quite striking. Elaborate Victorian chairs were slipcovered to simplify their form. An iron table looks almost like sculpture. Using an airy open table allows light to come into the room, a crucial consideration when walls are painted a dark color. The folding screen adds architectural interest while hiding a television.

ABOVE Although tartans are historically associated with Scotland, their colorful, complex geometric patterns can be enjoyed anywhere. Tartan is used extensively but never in an overwhelming way in this room—on the chairs, over the mirror, and on the table. Painted furniture helps the room feel less formal than it otherwise might. **OPPOSITE** An Egyptian-theme toile de Jouy under glass lends this side table a distinctive identity, as well as a bit of whimsy.

ABOVE White cuts any heaviness that might be associated with dark brown on its own. In this den, which gets a lot of sunlight, brown and white are combined with pale green. The dark window blind is reminiscent of the big mahogany shutters used in old colonial houses in the tropics. Polka-dot tapes make the blind more playful. **LEFT** A passageway or hall is always a good place to indulge a desire for dark colors, because it isn't a space where you will spend hours on end. Here, the white woodwork, the white shade on the sconce, and the white mats on the botanical prints nicely contrast with the deep reddish brown. The silver sconce and gilded frames further brighten the effect.

BELOW The heaviness of a chocolate-brown velvet sofa is balanced against lightness, provided here by daylight and by the delicacy of the objects arranged on the adjoining table. The sofa could seem monolithic and staid without the fillip of white piping on the pillow. The tabletop display includes a collection of glass bottles and pottery, valued more for their diverse shapes and colors than for their importance as art objects. The amber-colored glass also helps bring out the caramel tones in the brown upholstery.

ABOVE Sumptuous yet homey, this room shows the multitude of colors that exist within the spice palette. The beautifully worn paneled wall is rich in detail, as is the 1960s-style rug, with its geometric pattern making use of the spectrum of spice tones. The bedcover, too, plays with many browns. Along with the old mirror, shimmering fabrics on the pillows provide welcome patches of light. **OPPOSITE** When the darkest shades of brown predominate, it helps to add reflective or pale objects as a counterbalance. Here, pewter plates on the shelf and a silver frame supply that luminosity, making this corner moody but not dour.

BELOW Pale browns and creams with just a touch of color in the floor and on the bedside table produce a serene bedroom. The dark bedstead gets a fresh look from simple slipcovers: Panels of brown-and-white cotton ticking are sewn along the top rails to follow the profiles of the head- and footboard and then tied loosely at the sides. A small painted mirror, a painted chair, and a white lampshade also contribute to the clean, light atmosphere.

HANGING A CANOPY

You don't need a canopy bed to enjoy the charm of a canopy. This one, made of gingham-checked material, is fairly simple to assemble and hang, and it gives more prominence to your bed frame.

It is best to make this canopy with a double-sided fabric or a woven one, so that the pattern is the same on the front and the back. The width of the fabric should approximately match the width of the bed. To determine the fabric's length—which depends on the height of your ceiling—add the following measurements: the height of the canopy (approximately 6 to 7 feet); the length of your bed; and the length of the drop (the flap above the foot of the bed, approximately 18 inches). Finish all four edges of the fabric. To create pockets for two dowels 1¼ inches in diameter, cut two strips of the same fabric, making each strip 3½ inches wide and the same length as the width of the canopy. Turn under ½ inch on either edge of each strip, so that the finished width of each is 2½ inches. Stitch one strip, raw edges in, to the canopy along the line where the headboard panel meets the top and the other where the top of the canopy meets the drop. Slip 1¼-inch-diameter dowels into the pockets. The dowels should be as long as the canopy is wide. (Before inserting dowels, paint their ends a color that coordinates with your fabric, since they will be visible when in place.) Flip the canopy over so that the dowel pockets are on the underside. Screw brass eye hooks through the fabric and into the dowel from the top of the canopy approximately 6 inches from the ends of the dowels. Mark the ceiling directly above the four corners of your bed. Attach a screw eye to the ceiling at each of the four points. You will need to secure the eyes with an anchor appropriate to your ceiling construction, as they must support the weight of the canopy. Attach one end of a lightweight brass chain to each of the screw eyes on the canopy. Then attach the other end of each chain to a screw eye in the ceiling. You may have to experiment with the length of the chains until you are happy with the angle and drape of the canopy.

MATERIALS

fabric

dowels

paint

eye hooks

screw eyes

anchors

brass chains

If only we were as talented as the ocean, which takes our cast-off bottles and jars and magically turns them into sea glass. Few things are quite so rewarding as walking along the beach and glancing down to find one of these frosted, glowing jewels. Sea glass may be brown or red or white, but most memorable are the blue and green pieces. Increasingly, because plastic and aluminum containers have been replacing glass, sea glass is harder to find and therefore more coveted. In fact, there is now a demand for manmade sea glass, but no process can substitute for the random force of the ocean. Just as it transforms scrap timber into romantically sculpted driftwood, the surf picks up a bottle tossed on the beach, whips it around in the waves, breaks it apart, and smooths the jagged edges, giving each piece a soft, rounded shape. In the sun, the glass can remind us of shiny crystal; on a cloudy day, it looks more murky and gray, as if the sea itself has been captured inside, never to escape.

SEA GLASS

The colors in this palette are green blues and blue greens, like the waves in the ocean, with dark and light variations. Some contain a bit of gray, making them more reminiscent of waves on an overcast day. It is hard to overdo these shades; in fact, their beauty becomes more evident when a number of them are used at once. The palette works in formal or casual settings. Combined with sandy tones, the colors are moody; against sharp, clean whites, the look is crisp and nautical.

SWATCHES For this living room, opposite, the materials include subtle shades of blue and green. Blending is integral to this palette, largely because the goal is to create a sense of fluidity. The wood sample above represents the frame of the folding screen. The pale wood furniture, the subtle stripes of the folding screen, and the soft velvet fabrics, opposite, all share a washed-out, faded quality. Visual texture results from using some clean and bright colors with others that are gray. The lamp-shade, table, and rug are neutral, to offset the blues and greens.

OPPOSITE This room presents a formal interpretation of the palette in its palest, gentlest tones. Much of it is subtly reflective, from the dusty-gray silk-tufted fabric on the sofa to the mercury-glass lamp to the clear glass vase. White anemones and roses, mixed with hydrangeas and viburnum, play off the green side of sea glass, while the sand-colored carpet draws upon another range of tones familiar to any beachcomber. This pale version of the palette benefits from a flood of bright natural light through the tall Palladian window.

ABOVE The beautiful light in the room is enhanced by the soft and flowing fabrics of a silk-lined cashmere and wool throw with ruffles reminiscent of sea anemones, and curtains that are half cream linen, half turquoise taffeta. Filtered through the curtains, the light makes the room appear almost as if it were underwater. **LEFT** Do not underestimate the impact created by a variety of reflecting materials, like this array of water, glass, mirror, and polished metal. Fresh mint in the water adds splashes of green. With chairs covered in pale silvery blue, this room looks ready for a mermaid's cocktail party.

BELOW Here, the colors of the sea-glass palette are more subdued. With its early-1900s Sheraton-style sideboard, silver-plated sconces, and engraved portraits of George Washington, the room runs the risk of feeling too much like a period piece. It is brought up to date with the white painted chairs and the simple modern frames used on all the engravings. Bold touches of red in the porcelain bowl and the flowers tie this room to the one that can be seen beyond.

ABOVE This floor is covered in a mix of sun-faded blues, offset by white shutters. The blue of the galvanized metal stools inspired the rest of the palette, while the sandy-colored linen seat covers pull out the warm tones of the wooden table. RIGHT A predominantly white kitchen gains a layer of color when the cabinet interior is painted a pale blue. As an alternative, matching blue door curtains could continue the color scheme while also concealing the everyday kitchen necessities.

ABOVE This bathroom shows the softly luminous effects that can be achieved with this palette when sunlight pours into a room. The light coming through a window in the shower highlights the mirror, the jadeite boxes, the marble sink, and the glass sink legs. When sea-glass blues, greens, and grays are combined with white, they emphasize the clean lines of a spare contemporary room. Its sparseness is softened by the colors, rather than by decorative objects.

LEAF PRINTS

A collage of leaf prints lets you enjoy your garden all year long. The ink-rolling process picks up textural details in a way that photography cannot. More than just decorative, the prints create a journal of the season's hard work and tangible rewards.

Cut leaves, and preserve them in water. While leaves are still fresh, press them for half an hour before printing. If you don't have a flower press, improvise using a heavy phone book. 1. You'll need a smooth surface on which to work (a 10-by-12-inch piece of glass works best). Have a stack of paper handy: Basic book print will do, but feel free to experiment; we used pages of text featuring favorite garden poems. 2. Using a mini trowel, scoop out ink (you can use basic printmakers' ink in place of etching ink), and smear it on the glass. Roll a thin layer of ink on the glass with a brayer (a rubber roller available at art-supply stores). Using tweezers, place a pressed leaf, veined side down, on the inked surface, and smooth it out. Lay a sheet of waxed paper on top of the leaf. Roll over the waxed paper with a second dry brayer, applying enough pressure to ensure that the ink penetrates the leaf. Remove the waxed paper. 3. Pick up the leaf with the tweezers, and lay it, inked side down, on a sheet of paper. Take a clean piece of waxed paper, place on top of the leaf, and roll with the dry brayer. Remove the waxed paper and the leaf, leaving behind the impression. If desired, arrange prints on Foamcore or cardboard backing; attach them with archival tape; frame.

MATERIALS

leaves

flower press

glass surface

paper

mini trowel

etching ink

brayers

tweezers

waxed paper

People who consistently favor yellow are said to like motion, newness, and change. It is fitting then that many of the first flowers of spring, pushing up when the ground has barely thawed, are yellow, for these are the garden's har-bingers of change, letting us know that a new season has arrived. Of all the spring flowers, it is the daffodil, also known by its

JONQUIL

Latin name, *Narcissus*, that seems most emblematic of the season. Found in thousands of varieties, ranging from white to yellow to orange, it will grow nearly anywhere in the United States and Canada. It is an old-fashioned flower, but at the same time its simple form and bright color make it appear at home in any modern setting. One of our favorite varieties is the jonquil, which is character-ized by clusters of yellow flowers, a strong scent, and rounded foliage. Like every member of the daffodil family, the jonquil is a cheerful flower. Its color seems warm, as if the sun had agreed to share a little piece of itself to cheer up the creatures worn down by winter's gray days.

This palette extends from the palest to the most saturated yellows, with a hint of green reflecting the flower's stem. A small amount of yellow makes a grand statement; it's not like some of our other favorites, which benefit most from being used many times in a room. Yet, although yellow can easily overwhelm, devotees will find that it can be used successfully throughout certain rooms and in warm light for a crisp monochromatic look. Yellow teams easily with white, cream, and beige, providing a punch of color against a neutral background.

SWATCHES The neutrals of the rug and fabrics are balanced by yellow, used in several places in the room opposite to increase the brightening effect. Even the magazines stacked on the wicker desk in the background are the same color. The rag-style rug, a flat weave in a geometric pat- tern, contributes to the play of textures that helps keep this room interesting. The top paint chip above illustrates the color of the wall, a light tone that is countered by the dark wood floor. Overall, the jonquil palette ties together the room and its disparate flea-market furnishings.

OPPOSITE This predominantly beige-and-white color scheme relies on contrasting textures and a few bursts of yellow to create a lively yet relaxing corner. Chrome yellow paint on the Chippendale-style mirror provides a focal point, as do the full-blown roses. This is basically a neutral room enlivened with some strong yellow. It would be possible to transform it into a blue or green room just by changing the accents.

How much do you like yellow? These three rooms effectively use the color to varying degrees. **ABOVE** There is nothing tentative about this room. From the lemons to the mantel to the walls, it is yellow all the way. And yet, oddly enough, yellow functions like a neutral, becoming a backdrop for the boldly painted green mirror on the wall. **LEFT** An assortment of yellow objects brightens a dark corner. Most colors look good paired with their opposite on the color wheel, and yellow is no exception; here, yellow in the vases harmonizes well with its opposite, the purple in the striped pitcher. **OPPOSITE** If you like yellow but want to confine your passion to one section of a room, consider painting a single piece of furniture. This bureau, a battered piece found at a flea market, was painted in two shades of yellow, one on the frame and the other outlining the details. As in the garden, yellow and green make an agreeable match, in the framed print and the bouquet of flowers.

LEFT In this room, yellow is paired with white and tends toward the soft tints of butter and cream. The yellow in the pillowcase picks up the yellow woven into the bedspread, and the creamy yellow on the window frames emphasizes their curving lines. The throw at the end of the bed, with its deep-yellow stripes, gives the room a gentle jolt. Grandly presiding over all is the chandelier, the object that inspired the creation of the rest of the room. Because the entire room uses the same palette, there is no competition for attention. **BELOW** There's a childlike innocence to a sunny yellow. These children's drawings, matted in a strong yellow, add one of the few notes of color to this all-white summer-house kitchen complete with vintage sink and wooden drainboards.

project

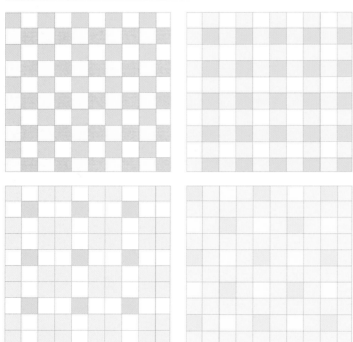

Each pattern above comprises no more than three shades of color, including white or gray, in combinations that use only whole (uncut) tiles.

This patterned tile floor is linoleum, but you could use ceramic, wood, or another material and vary the colors. Keep in mind, however, that a higher-contrast palette will produce a busier effect.

Look to favorite tile arrangements, window patterns, fabric designs, or even quilts for inspiration for your floor. Whether the design you choose is random or perfectly symmetrical, keep in mind the size of the room. A tightly focused pattern and a lighter palette will make a small room seem larger. Vivid colors may distract your eye from the boxiness of a room, but they can also make it look smaller. Use colors of the same family to create tonal harmonies. Or consider introducing one tile from the opposite side of the color wheel into a unified range of tones to provide an accent and add contrast to the mix. And when choosing your palette, make sure the transition from one room to the next is not jarring. Floor patterns can be created with tiles of many materials, including vinyl, ceramics, and wood. For durability, we like linoleum, an environmentally friendly floor covering made of linseed oil (derived from flax), resins, cork powder, wood or limestone flour, and pigment. Linoleum comes in two forms: in hefty rolls of a single color and in twelve-inch tiles.

MATERIALS

tiles

photocopier

glue stick

ABOVE LEFT **1.** Start by going to a flooring store and picking tile samples in colors you like. To choose your color combination, play off existing colors in the room, and then simplify. **2.** Photocopy the tile samples on a color copier. Cut the copies into uniformly sized squares, using a scale of about one inch to one foot. Make enough copies so you can experiment with patterns and color combinations. **3.** Paste the photocopied squares into grids with a glue stick, repeating each pattern at least twice. The same three colors can create very different rhythms, depending on where the darkest and lightest tiles are used or where neutrals, such as white or gray, are introduced. In the example on the top left, gray tones down the palette, so the yellow doesn't pop out as it would if paired with only white and cream. **4.** Draw a plan of the entire floor, laying it out on a grid keyed to scale. This will help you figure out where the center of your design will fall; how to treat its borders, which may not be completely symmetrical; and how many tiles to order. A plastic sleeve protects the grid, which can also serve as a guide for the installer. Laying linoleum tile is easier than installing ceramic or wood tile, because the material is more pliable and less fragile. But it does take patience and exactitude, so it's best to hire a professional. Schedule the project for warm weather, because cold air can harden linoleum, sometimes making it brittle enough to snap.

ABOVE Using large pale squares of linoleum in shades of yellow and cream creates a calming and practical solution for this kitchen floor. Hints of yellow in the yellowware bowls, dishcloths, kitchen crockery, and even the garden roses tie the floor to the rest of the room, unifying the space.

Green in its many guises is a restful, comforting, versatile color that, like blue, has untold fans. Look out the window, and you may see many shades of green, from the acid green of a coleus to the deep blue green of a spruce. One shade we find particularly inspiring is celadon, the color of a pottery originally from China that we have collected for many

CELADON

years. Celadon was first produced during the period known as the Song Dynasty, between 960 and 1279. Its Chinese name, *qingci,* means "greenish porcelain." The pottery became known as celadon in seventeenth-century Europe, most likely in reference to the hero of the French pastoral romance novel *L'Astrée,* published in 1610. Céladon, a shepherd, was noted for his green clothing, a style much imitated in Europe at about the same time the Chinese pottery was being introduced to Paris. Many centuries later, the pottery is still winning new admirers, who are drawn to its simple shapes as well as its colors, which range from gray green to olive to jade.

The definition of celadon is hard to pin down. The purest celadon is a very gray green, but the name may refer to any of a range of dusty, blue-gray greens. The same palette can also incorporate yellow and gray-blue tones. Throughout a room, you can use shades of one tone or mix several successfully. Celadon is extraordinarily sensitive to light. Painted in a corner bookcase, any shade will seem much darker than when the same color is painted on a flat surface near a window.

SWATCHES Faux bamboo furniture in the bedroom opposite provides warm tones that work well to offset the many cool shades of celadon. The lacy linens and the curvilinear armchair balance the bony profile of the bamboo bedstead and folding screen and the angular geometry of the star-pattern quilt. The subtler texture of the cotton faille bedspread creates a quiet foil. The effectiveness of combining several different shades of celadon is demonstrated in this room, whose mix of blue, green, and yellow tones creates richness and complexity.

OPPOSITE These shades of green complement the faux bamboo bed and folding screen in part because the colors remind us of the mix of leaf and wood tones so often found in nature. The greens used here also work to harmonize an eclectic mix of furniture—the chair is eighteenth-century French, the hooked rug is from the twentieth century, and the quilt is classic Americana. The beautifully aged mirror on the wall has lost much of its ability to reflect, but its rounded frame provides an effective contrast to the extremely rectilinear furniture.

Celadon is a good choice when you are looking for a color that is barely there to go with whites and creams. These three rooms benefit from touches of color without losing any of their subtlety. **OPPOSITE** A headboard found at a flea market was given a fresh coat of paint and upholstered with celadon linen. The textured white spread reflects the patterns of sunlight, but the only permanent pattern in the room is the tattersall check on the pillowcases. On the table, a celadon vase and bowl typify the artfully simple, classic shapes that define the pottery. **ABOVE** White marble countertops, like the island in this kitchen, can seem chilly without the added warmth of color. Here, under-the-counter cabinets are painted celadon, and overhead cabinets are trimmed in the same tone. This color works particularly well with stainless-steel appliances. **RIGHT** A bathroom decorated in shades of gold, beige, and white receives hints of celadon from a vase, towels, and soap.

BELOW On the lively geometric wall of this kitchen, the lattice is a light shade of celadon, and the background is a darker one. The color is similar to that of the Frankoma pottery the owner collects, arranged on the shelf above. The reddish oranges of the flowers and the framed still life link this room to the orange hallway beyond. **RIGHT** A medium-toned celadon won't show every scratch, so the color is perfect for this mudroom with its functional pegs for coats. It also keeps the room feeling light and airy, an important consideration in a space such as this, which can easily seem cluttered.

ABOVE When choosing a palette for a porch, look for colors that reflect the tones of the landscape, so that these areas visually connect. The glass-enclosed porch at Turkey Hill centers on a table surrounded by wicker chairs that received a coat of pale celadon paint. The particular color was inspired by the ferns on the pedestals, which were made from old fluted columns. However, even when the ferns are removed, the celadon furniture gracefully reflects the variety of greens outdoors.

COMBED GINGHAM DRAWERS

Once you try the simple technique of combing on one piece of furniture, you will want to apply it to more. In addition to creating a pretty grid pattern on a chest of drawers (right), combing can dress up the back wall of a bookcase or the interior of a china closet.

To create a gingham look on a dresser, first apply a base coat. Use latex paint with a low-luster finish. **1.** When the base coat is dry, use painter's tape to mask a border on the front of each drawer. To make the glaze, combine 2 ounces of an oil-based paint—in a complementary or contrasting color to the base coat—and 2 ounces of paint thinner, and stir with a small brush until thoroughly dissolved. Add 4 ounces of an alkyd glaze finish (available in hardware or paint stores), and continue to mix until blended. Apply a thin layer of the glaze over the base coat, and remove any excess with a lint-free cloth or dry brush. **2.** Place a T-square on the drawer panel so that its short edge is parallel to the short edge—or height—of the panel. You can use an ordinary T-square or create your own with two pieces of wood. If the T-square lies on the surface, it can smudge the effect—prop it up on small, thin pieces of wood such as chopsticks. While the glaze is wet, place a combing tool (available at paint stores) against the side of the T-square. To make your own comb, cut teeth with a utility knife into any rigid material, such as plastic or rubber. Pull the teeth toward you—along the length of the panel—in a smooth and even motion, creating narrow lines in the finish. After each pass, wipe the comb clean of excess paint, and gently slide the T-square over to where the next set of lines will be, making sure that each set is evenly spaced. **3.** When the first layer has dried thoroughly, paint a second layer of glaze over the panel. Place the T-square across the shorter edge of the drawer—perpendicular to the first set of lines—and pull the comb down. Slide the T-square over and repeat until the pattern is complete.

MATERIALS

latex paint

painter's tape

oil-based paint

paint thinner

alkyd glaze

cloth or brush

T-square

combing tool

DRILLED SWAG HEADBOARD

Drill dimpled designs into a headboard before painting it. Our swag pattern was created with a countersink bit, which makes a mark like the impression left in wet sand by a fingertip.

First, sand and prime the wood, then place it on a stable base, such as sawhorses or a workbench, so that you can operate the drill at a comfortable working height. **1.** Before drilling, sketch your design on a roll of tracing paper; then use a plastic circle template (available at art-supply stores) to mark the areas to be countersunk. Coat the paper lightly and evenly with spray adhesive, then press onto wood. Avoid working on rainy days, when humidity can cause the paper to pucker. **2.** Since a gradation of hole sizes, as in the swags below, is produced with a single ⅝-inch bit (see page 18), practice is key. Drill through the circles with a light, brief touch to leave a shallow dimple; a heavier, longer touch results in a deeper, wider imprint. Apply paint to the headboard with stiff dabs to reach every cranny, then smooth out with a swiping motion.

MATERIALS

tracing paper
circle template
spray adhesive
drill
countersink bit
paint

Many birds are more brilliantly colored than the dove. When the peacock spreads its plumage, the array of blues and greens is stunning, and a bright-red cardinal in the garden always merits a second look. Most doves, however, do not announce their presence with such obvious fanfare. Rather, they blend into their surroundings, with feathers in subtle

DOVE

shades of gray and white, iridescent brown, pearl, and even pale tangerine. In fact, it is hard to describe the exact color of a dove. In the shade of a large, leafy tree, it might seem gray, but in direct sunlight the same bird can appear to be many colors simultaneously. The colors of this palette are atmospheric, moody, and elusive, like the bird itself, which has been known to escape the grip of a human hand by simply shedding most of its feathers, slipping away, and flying to safety. But however hard it may be to capture, this is the bird chosen by people around the world to symbolize one of the most challenging and important ideals of our day, or any day: the hope of peace.

Like white or beige, gray is a neutral that can take on many guises, with overtones of brown or blue or even pink. Gray can tend toward silver or lead, but its character depends enormously on the light. In a northern light it will grow chilly, but direct sunlight renders it warm and embracing. Similarly, gray-browns appear golden in certain lights but simply muddy in others. Because it is difficult even for an expert to distinguish between a warm gray and a cold one on a sample chip, be sure to paint swatches on the wall before selecting a specific shade.

SWATCHES These materials, all used in the dining room on the opposite page, present a balance of warm and cool shades of dove. Mahogany furniture is warm with a red hue, while the blue on the ceiling and on the chairs is cool. The creamy white painted trim keeps the balance of the room from shifting too heavily toward cool. The softly patterned carpet contributes yellow and golden tones, as do the bouquet of roses on the mantel and the pyramid of peaches in the center of the table. The latter tones are represented above by the ribbon tying the swatches together.

OPPOSITE The gray walls in this formal room are so dramatic that you don't have to hang much on them. A wall color like this is pleasingly moody at night, which makes it well suited to a dining room. Fruit and flower arrangements provide dramatic bits of color, and because they are temporary, their colors can be varied from one week to the next, easily changing the feel of the room.

Whether pale or dark, dove gray looks good when paired with white. **BELOW** A dark gray background makes artwork matted in white pop off the wall. The stark white moldings and stair balusters also provide contrast, creating a strong statement in a hallway—a space whose decorative potential tends to be overlooked. **OPPOSITE, TOP** A warm gray outlines sand-colored walls, creating a smoky, almost misty atmosphere. The hallway beyond uses muslin white on the walls, luring the eye through the doorway. **BOTTOM RIGHT** Sparkly objects—such as this mirror and chandelier—look especially pretty against muted shades of gray. **BOTTOM LEFT** Red and gray are a classic combination. Here, a dining room with red walls, a red table, and even red plates leads into a hallway that is painted dove. The hallway is visually tied to the dining room with an arrangement of red flowers, a red porcelain Chinese garden stool, and a carpet with red highlights.

A narrow range of the dove palette looks sophisticated when different patterns or textures are introduced. **OPPOSITE** A soft striped fabric behind each headboard counteracts the chill of the silvery blue gray. The warm, worn pine floor is the perfect foil for the cool blue-gray rug. **ABOVE LEFT** This room is reminiscent of a black-and-white photograph, with its simple yet carefully composed sense of contrast. The gray wall is set off with luminous white bedding and curtains, allowing the strong, graphic lines of the dark polished wood furniture to stand out. **ABOVE RIGHT** Warm grays and creamy, light-catching fabrics suit a sunny corner. A geometric rug repeats the color scheme and the clean, modern lines of the daybed. Flat panels of organza filter the daylight.

ATMOSPHERIC CANDLES

Make beeswax candles, and arrange a grouping on a table indoors. Cover them with metal mesh hurricanes, and they deliver a golden glow. Set outside, their flames will be protected from the evening breeze.

BEESWAX CANDLES These pillars combine the appeal of beeswax with the sturdiness of an interior pillar. Beeswax sheets can be purchased at candle-making shops. Cut a sheet to the height and circumference of the pillar. If the sheet feels stiff and brittle, make it more pliable by warming it with a hair dryer. Wrap the sheet around the pillar, then press the two edges together to seal. Place the seam in back when arranging the pillars for display.

MATERIALS
pillar candles
beeswax sheets

MESH HURRICANES These hurricanes are made of mesh sheets and matching metal thread in brass, bronze, and copper. To determine the width of the hurricane, measure the circumference of a pillar candle; add ½ inch for overlap. The hurricane should be 2 or 3 inches taller than the candle. Cut mesh to these dimensions.

MATERIALS
pillar candles
mesh sheets
bone folder
T-pin
metal thread

1. With a bone folder and a straightedge, fold top and bottom of mesh over ½ inch. Crease sharply with the bone folder. Form the hurricane by sliding top and bottom folds into one another. **2**. To keep the cylinder from buckling, make two holes in the overlapped side with a T-pin. Draw metal thread through the holes; tie and cut. Tall hurricanes may need to be tied in two or three places.

Like the familiar glass hurricanes that have long sheltered candles, these mesh cylinders surround pillars to protect the flame. The mesh adds a complex pattern to the candlelight. For a flameproof base, the candles are set on slabs of stone found at flea markets. We glued felt on the bottom of the stone to protect the table.

Is there a child who hasn't held a shell to her ear to listen to the sound of the ocean? This early discovery leaves us with a sense of wonder. Thus imprinted in our memory, the conch, one of nature's most enchanting creations, repeatedly inspires and moves us with its shape and color. The conch shell's complex form makes it an excellent, if primitive, horn, but even more exciting is its color, which runs from deepest pink to whitest white and sometimes includes shades of brown and beige. The shell, which we see as simply a beautiful object, actually serves an important protective function as the exterior skeleton of a mollusk. The mollusk builds the shell from calcium carbonate taken from food or seawater, and the shell expands as the mollusk does. The variety of color that we so admire reflects changes in the mollusk's diet or the water's composition. The colors are made even more complex by variations in the texture of the shell, from smooth to ridged to rough, much like coral, another wondrous marvel of sea life.

CONCH SHELL

COOL SHADES

HOT ACCENTS

PEACHY SHADES

ANTIQUE SHADES

Pink results from mixing red with white, but whereas red is a demanding hue that makes a powerful statement, pink can be far more subtle and varied. Although pink is often associated with little girls and things feminine, adults make a mistake in too often bypassing this color. When paired with white, it is fresh. With darker neutrals, such as beige, khaki, and olive brown, it looks sophisticated and elegant. Pink gives the darker colors some life, and they in turn offset its sweetness.

SWATCHES The collection of pinks and whites used in the bedroom opposite has only one accent color, a strong dash of green provided by the geranium in the window. Pink paint was applied to every inch of the wall and ceiling, minimizing the angles of the dormer. The pink and white fabrics shown above mimic the tints in the vintage quilted bedspread, opposite, found at a flea market in Paris. Pink and white are further balanced in the room by the browns of the old pine chair and the rug, made from sea grass. These carpets are green when they are initially woven but become brown as the sea grasses dry out.

OPPOSITE This small attic guest room, furnished very simply with a bed and a chair, is an enveloping retreat. Even the artwork is an homage to its surroundings' dominant color; the small framed drawings depict the flowers known as pinks (*Dianthus*). Although a salmon pink has been liberally applied on the wall and the coverlet, the color does not overwhelm, thanks in part to the neutral brown carpet.

OPPOSITE Touches of pink bring out hints of red in the brown furniture, the walls, and the curtains in this room. Pink is most effective in the niches, where it gives the otherwise somber room a lift. Gilding on the Queen Anne–style chinoiserie side chair and the sconce further brightens the room. The acid-green leaves of the plant look particularly fresh and focus the eye, as does the mirrored coffee table. **LEFT** The monochromatic application of pink in this room, from the walls to the flowers to the tea set, is brought into sharp relief by the dark wood of the table and chair. The pale-pink organza shade over the window delicately filters the light. **BELOW LEFT** Pink adds gentle warmth to a nearly all-white room. Here, a pink toile duvet was covered with voile, softening the color and making it more romantic. **BELOW** Although it may look very different from the living room on the facing page, this room uses the same colors—green, pink, and brown—but in their most muted expressions. The pale-pink cabinet against the pale-green wall modifies the classic combination of red and green.

LEFT This predominantly neutral room derives much of its visual interest from texture, created by the interplay of the horizontal paneling on the wall, the rafters overhead, the rattan chairs, the wicker basket, and the sea-grass carpet. The neutral combination of beige, brown, and white warms up with the addition of pinks, from the throw on the back of the sofa to the striped pillow to the cushion on the wooden armchair. Pink was even used to line the white window shades, giving the sunlight a rosy glow. Such details give the room levity without going so far as to make it silly. The dark frames, the black tin lanterns, and even the black standing lamp punctuate the airy color scheme. **BELOW** Anyone looking for the right pink should study this collection, which shows the range expressed by this color as well as its popularity over the centuries. Pink is not a trendy or modern color, nor an old and fussy one; these pieces date from the Victorian era to the end of the twentieth century. There are pinks so pale they almost disappear, as well as pinks that veer toward orange, brown, and red.

BELOW One can indulge a love of pink without committing to paint or upholstery. Here, it is used in a temperate way, as an accent rather than as the dominant tone. On the table, a simple square pink cloth is placed over a white one. Pink tones also show up in the antique copper molds that serve as a centerpiece, and in the plates and glasses. **RIGHT** Another transitory use of pink is in this eclectic tablesetting, which uses plates and glasses both contemporary and antique. The color helps unify objects from different periods. This setting also brings to life two familiar color combinations: pink and yellow, as seen in the antique French porcelain plate; and pink and brown, in the napkin and the charger.

ABOVE At Turkey Hill, a neutral-colored room becomes pink for one night. The zinc-coated copper table is set with silver lustreware, drabware, pearl-handled flatware, and centerpieces of garden roses and peonies. For another dinner, the room could be mostly green or blue or yellow, depending on the china, linens, and flowers.

BELOW A nautical pink toile in a guest room covers the bed's headboard, footboard, and a nearby screen. White in the furniture, linens, and lampshade prevents the toile from overpowering the small space. Toile is one of Martha's favorite patterns. The designs appeal to adults because of historical references in the imagery; children like toile because it seems to have many stories to tell.

Sometimes a bedroom needs a detail or two to pull it together or to make it seem special. Here, a white pillowcase is given a gingham trim, and a small accent pillow is monogrammed in cross-stitch.

PILLOWCASE CUFF To make a 4-inch-wide cuff for a pillowcase, cut two 5-inch-wide strips of gingham 1½ inches longer than the perimeter of the pillowcase's opening. **1.** Pin rickrack to the right side of one strip, so the center of the rickrack is ½ inch from the edge; stitch in place along the center. Lay the second long strip of gingham on top of the first, so right sides are facing. Stitch together along first seam. **2.** Turn the piece right side out, revealing the rickrack; press. Sew the short ends of the strip together (forming a circle), to make a cuff the same size as the pillowcase opening. Turn one raw edge of the cuff under ½ inch, and press. Slip the cuff onto the pillowcase so the unpressed edge is flush with the opening of the pillowcase and right sides are facing. Then stitch the gingham cuff to the pillowcase with a ½-inch seam allowance. Bring the folded edge to the inside of the pillowcase; slip-stitch layers of cuff and pillowcase together, and topstitch if desired.

MONOGRAMMED PILLOWCASE Gingham provides a ready-made template for cross-stitching a monogram: Simply fill in the boxes. Sketch your monogram on grid paper, and then lightly copy the template in pencil onto a gingham pillowcase before beginning to sew. To make a cross-stitch, first stitch a row of evenly spaced diagonal lines. Then stitch diagonally back over the first row, creating crosses as you go. Use the same holes when possible. Bottom stitches should all slant in one direction and top stitches in the other.

MATERIALS

- pillowcases
- gingham fabric
- rickrack
- embroidery thread
- grid paper

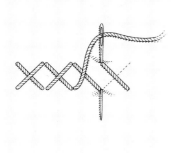

CROSS-STITCH

We have created these additional palettes to go along with our color chapters. They will give you more ideas about how to mix colors, textures, and materials, further inspiring you to create rooms that are easy, comfortable, and beautiful.

PALETTE 2 Creamy tones to warm up ironstone. **1.** Smith + Noble window blinds, Natural Pine, 270. **2.** Brunschwig & Fils, Baldwin Texture, White, 3251.01/0. **3.** Martha Stewart Everyday Colors, Ursa Major, H23. **4.** Rogers & Goffigon, Denton Park, Magnolia, 802001-04. **5.** Martha Stewart Everyday Colors, Autumn Clematis, H20.

PALETTE 3 Ironstone with a pink cast, teamed with warm browns. **1.** Christopher Norman, Maintenon Strie, Beige, N-225-02. **2.** Fine Paints of Europe, the Skylands Colors, Trillium, 3. **3.** Pickled ash flooring. **4.** Glant, the Island Collection, Island Micro Chenille, 9610. **5.** Fine Paints of Europe, the Skylands Colors, Shadbush, 2. **6.** Hinson wall covering, 16322.

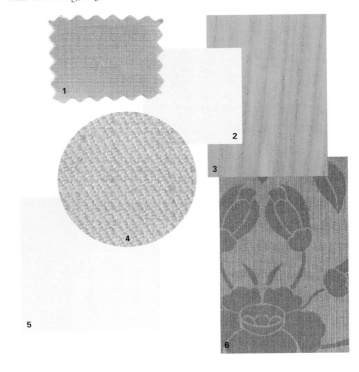

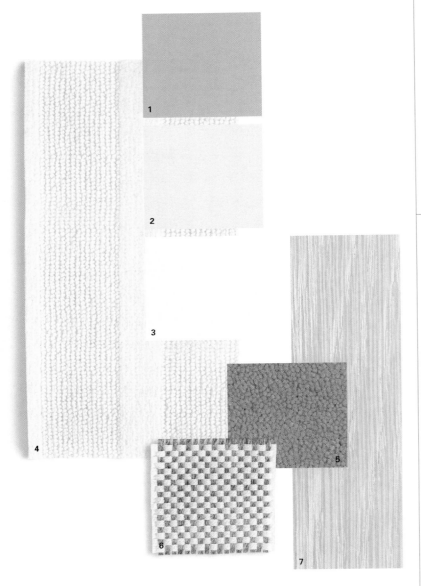

PALETTE 1 Ironstone in beige/neutral tones for a natural, sun-bleached feeling. **1.** Martha Stewart Signature, Pale Earth, 8076. **2.** Martha Stewart Signature, Rope, 8021. **3.** Martha Stewart Signature, Full Sail, 8022. **4.** Hinson, Deerfield Epingle, Off White, HCW64700-WF0. **5.** Masland, Landscape, Dolphin, 7218-410. **6.** Schumacher, Gianni, Linen, 92531. **7.** Whitewashed, cerused oak.

PALETTE 1 Stormy gray-blue textures combined with cool browns. **1.** Fine Paints of Europe, the Skylands Colors, Princess Wu, 35. **2.** Pollack, Rush Hour, Steel Blue, 5026/04. **3.** Dark cerused oak flooring. **4.** Rogers & Goffigon, Fiorella, Corot, 92902–06. **5.** Rose Tarlow, Melrose House, Velour Cord, Baltic, 2033/04. **6.** Fine Paints of Europe, the Skylands Colors, Delphinium Belladonna, 28. **7.** Classic Cloth, Ismelda, Mesquite, 1040-03.

PALETTE 2 Seaside blue with sandy accents. **1.** Martha Stewart Signature, Curlew, 8108. **2.** Rogers & Goffigon, Barksdale II, Loire, 910021-01. **3.** Martha Stewart Signature, Fresco, 8257.

PALETTE 3 Crisp blue and white warmed with natural sisal and pale wood. **1.** Natural ash flooring. **2.** Pratt & Lambert, Washed Denim, POR-1240-000. **3.** Pratt & Lambert, Coy Pink, POR-1240-000. **4.** Wool-and-sisal floor covering. **5.** Martha Stewart Signature, Glazed Metis, Blue, MSH-00098F. **6.** Christopher Norman, Ascot Plaid, Blue, N-221-05. **7.** Hinson, Carinthia, Blue, HCF-45001-B00.

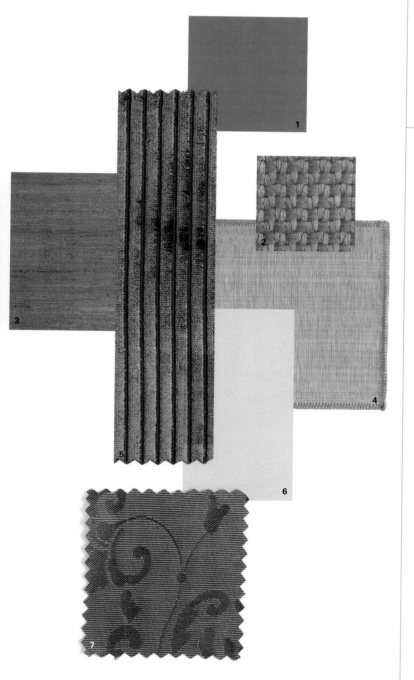

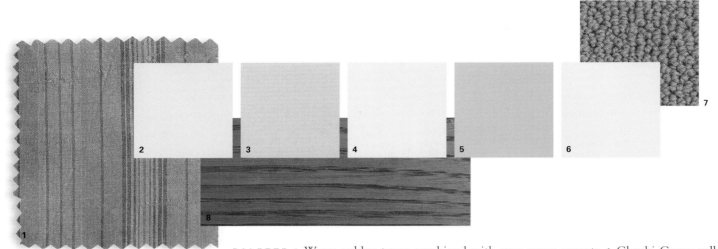

PALETTE 1 Warm golden tones combined with gray-green accents. **1**. Chechi Como yellow-and-gray silk. **2**. Martha Stewart Signature, Rattan, 8145. **3**. Martha Stewart Signature, Golden Pearl, 8150. **4**. Martha Stewart Signature, Chopstick, 8141. **5**. Martha Stewart Signature, Silt, 8114. **6**. Martha Stewart Signature, Hemp, 8106. **7**. Masland, Landscape, Wheat, 7218-261. **8**. Antique chestnut flooring.

PALETTE 2 Golden green hues. **1**. Benjamin Moore, Color Preview, Henderson Buff, HC-15. **2**. Benjamin Moore, Color Preview, Wethersfield Moss, HC-110. **3**. Benjamin Moore, Color Preview, Fernwood Green, 2145-40. **4**. Rogers & Goffigon, Denton Park, Yarrow, 802001-03.

PALETTE 3 Cool pinky naturals and warm golden neutrals accented with lavender. **1**. Fine Paints of Europe, the Araucana Colors, Golden Campine, 11. **2**. Ralph Lauren Home, Sutherland Herringbone, Hemp, LCF18206F. **3**. Benjamin Moore, Color Preview, Mauve Blush, 2115-40. **4**. Fine Paints of Europe, the Araucana Colors, Partridge Rock Brown, 12. **5**. Smith + Noble window blinds, Rustic Pine, 250.

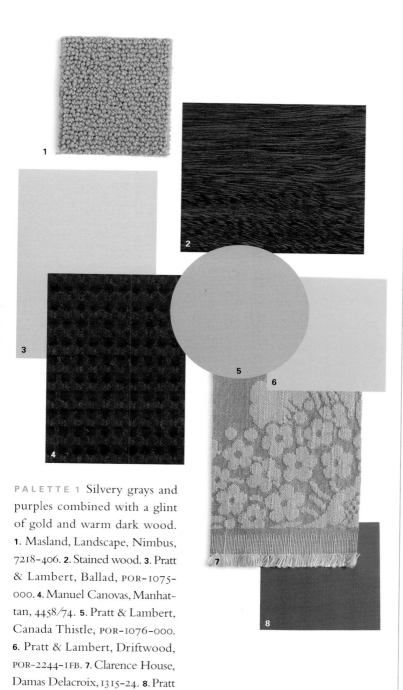

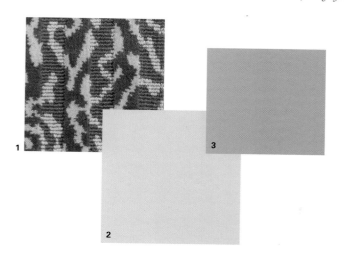

PALETTE 2 Purple warmed by reddish neutrals. **1.** Hines, Safari, Taupe, 1802-2. **2.** Benjamin Moore, Color Preview, Monroe Bisque, HC-26. **3.** Benjamin Moore, Color Preview, Mauve Desert, 2113-50.

PALETTE 1 Silvery grays and purples combined with a glint of gold and warm dark wood. **1.** Masland, Landscape, Nimbus, 7218-406. **2.** Stained wood. **3.** Pratt & Lambert, Ballad, POR-1075-000. **4.** Manuel Canovas, Manhattan, 4458/74. **5.** Pratt & Lambert, Canada Thistle, POR-1076-000. **6.** Pratt & Lambert, Driftwood, POR-2244-1FB. **7.** Clarence House, Damas Delacroix, 1315-24. **8.** Pratt & Lambert, Pale Aubergine, POR-1084-000.

PALETTE 3 Misty lavender gray with a hint of mint. **1.** Manuel Canovas, Ondine II, 4402-73. **2.** Martha Stewart Everyday, Thyme Flower, B09. **3.** Martha Stewart Everyday, Winter Surf, G23. **4.** Drift-wood gray flooring.

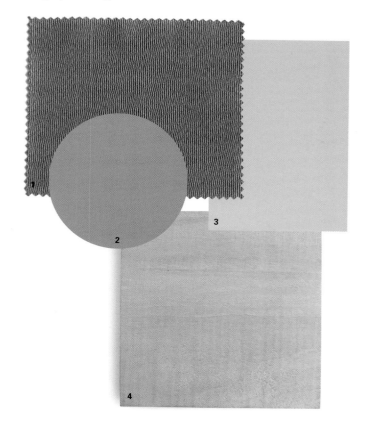

PALETTE 1 Pale melons mixed with textured neutrals. **1.** Pratt & Lambert, Split Pea, POR-1636-000. **2.** Bamboo flooring. **3.** Martha Stewart Everyday Colors, Butternut, E13. **4.** Rogers & Goffigon, Bechamel, Mantis, 938001-20. **5.** Pratt & Lambert, Yellow Chiffon, POR-1740-000. **6.** Pratt & Lambert, Dominique, POR-1852-000. **7.** Martha Stewart Everyday Colors, Sunflower, E10. **8.** Pollack, Rush Hour, Straw, 5026/01.

PALETTE 2 Hot melon cooled with green. **1.** Benjamin Moore, Color Preview, Salmon Peach, 2013-50. **2.** Manuel Canovas, Cotton Club, 4275/09. **3.** Fine Paints of Europe, the Skylands Colors, Flower Room, 26B. **4.** Benjamin Moore, Color Preview, Hibiscus, 2027-50.

PALETTE 3 Warm melons with a touch of yellow. **1.** Smith + Noble window blinds, Red Cedar, 781. **2.** Benjamin Moore, Color Preview, Morning Sunshine, 2018-50. **3.** Martha Stewart Signature, Gaugin, 8370. **4.** Clarence House, Damask Croquille Rose, 14153-ROSE. **5.** Manuel Canovas, Cotton Club, 4275/23.

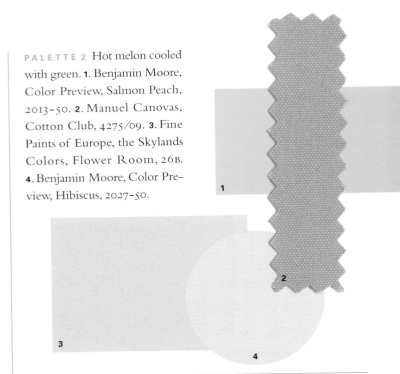

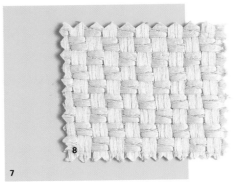

PALETTE 2 Rosy spice that plays up the pinks. **1.** Mulberry; Woven Caspar; Soft Pink, Green, and Gold, FD035/561 W108. **2.** Benjamin Moore, Color Preview, Livingston Gold, HC-16. **3.** Patterson, Flynn, & Martin, Asti, Camisole, 4263. **4.** Bergamo Fabrics, Marquis, 3725.

PALETTE 3 Deep spice with plummy undertones. **1.** Benjamin Moore, Color Preview, Hosbrouck Brown, HC-71. **2.** Benjamin Moore, Color Preview, Quincy Tan, HC-25. **3.** East Indian rosewood flooring. **4.** Rogers & Goffigon, Kells, Walnut, 92004-05. **5.** Pollack, Lotus, Antique, 2046/01.

PALETTE 1 Golden spice with hints of green. **1.** Martha Stewart Everyday, Wildflower Honey, E03. **2.** Clarence House, Mulberry Leaf, Beige, 33642-4. **3.** Larsen Carpet, Ruckstuhl, Dark Taupe, 1042/15. **4.** Martha Stewart Signature, Sourdough, 8014. **5.** Martha Stewart Signature, Fell, 8159. **6.** Honey oak wood flooring. **7.** Rogers & Goffigon, Posy, Senna, 805002-04. **8.** Martha Stewart Signature, Horsehair, 8157.

PALETTE 1 The beach on a stormy day—a gray sea glass. **1.** Masland, Landscape, Cream, 7218-304. **2.** Martha Stewart Signature Fabrics, Woodland Canopy, Azure, 1021. **3.** Benjamin Moore, Color Preview, Woodlawn Blue, HC-147. **4.** Benjamin Moore, Color Preview, Wythe Blue, HC-143. **5.** Rogers & Goffigon, Shaker, Blithe, 92509-05. **6.** Benjamin Moore, Color Preview, Windham Cream, HC-6. **7.** Rogers & Goffigon, Furrows, Glacier, 92514-06.

PALETTE 2 Quiet seas—a pale, elegant rendition of sea glass. **1.** Martha Stewart Everyday Colors, Glass Green, D20. **2.** Martha Stewart Everyday Colors, Lichen, D26. **3.** Old World Weavers, Bengali, Celeste, Silk, BA02240020. **4.** Martha Stewart Everyday Colors, Beach Glass, D24.

PALETTE 3 Sun and sand—clear colors and warm, sandy neutrals. **1.** Pratt & Lambert, Pacific, POR-1355-00. **2.** Bleached limed oak flooring. **3.** Pratt & Lambert, Oasis, POR-1408-000. **4.** Pratt & Lambert, Bird's Egg, POR-1334-000. **5.** Cowtan & Tout, Chiltern, Pale Aqua, F2110-14. **6.** Pratt & Lambert, Azurean, POR-01372-000.

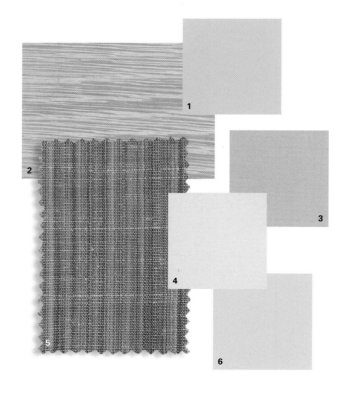

PALETTE 1 Strong, clear yellows with citrusy green accents.
1. Donghia, Stella, Luminary Yellow, 03. **2.** Martha Stewart Signature, Tomatillo, 8215. **3.** Martha Stewart Signature, Madeline, 8166.
4. Martha Stewart Signature, Green Apple, 8198. **5.** Martha Stewart Signature, Van Gogh, 8174. **6.** Martha Stewart Signature, Plantain, 8177. **7.** Crucial Trading, Light Honey Bouclé, Sisal, C581.

PALETTE 2 Softest yellow and blue set off by pale gray. **1.** Fine Paints of Europe, the Skylands Colors, Sea Lavender, 27. **2.** Gray stained ash veneer. **3.** Fine Paints of Europe, the Skylands Colors, Morning Warbler, 25.

PALETTE 3 Classic yellow and chocolate accented by purple.
1. Martha Stewart Everyday Colors, Thyme Flower, B09. **2.** Cowtan & Tout, Delafield Damask, Topaz, 10577-07. **3.** Martha Stewart Everyday Colors, Scone, H06. **4.** Masland, Landscape, Alabaster, 7218-373. **5.** Martha Stewart Everyday Colors, Black Bread, F02.

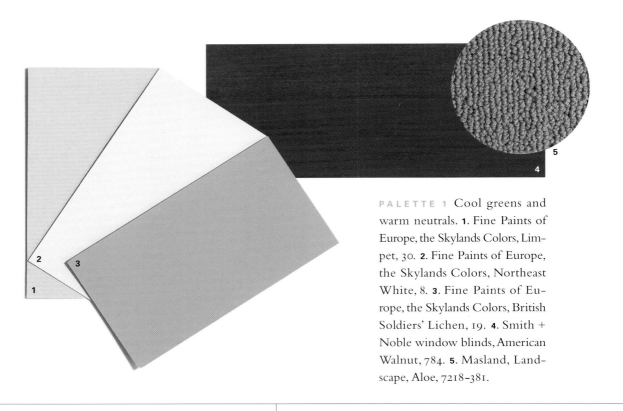

PALETTE 1 Cool greens and warm neutrals. **1.** Fine Paints of Europe, the Skylands Colors, Limpet, 30. **2.** Fine Paints of Europe, the Skylands Colors, Northeast White, 8. **3.** Fine Paints of Europe, the Skylands Colors, British Soldiers' Lichen, 19. **4.** Smith + Noble window blinds, American Walnut, 784. **5.** Masland, Landscape, Aloe, 7218-381.

PALETTE 2 Gray-greens plus warm wood. **1.** Smith + Noble window blinds, Karatsu Natural, 942. **2.** Benjamin Moore, Color Preview, Castleton Mist, HC-1. **3.** Benjamin Moore, Color Preview, Old Salem Gray, HC-94. **4.** Hinson, Pebbles Chenille, Celadon/Cream, HCW63700-GD0.

PALETTE 3 Celadons so pale as to be almost neutrals mixed with their complement, lavender. **1.** Martha Stewart Signature, Baby Blanket, 8101. **2.** Martha Stewart Signature, Blue John, 8348. **3.** Martha Stewart Signature, Dried Fava, 8112. **4.** Martha Stewart Signature, Beehive, 8107. **5.** Seagrass matting. **6.** Classic Cloth, Damask Villa, Erba.

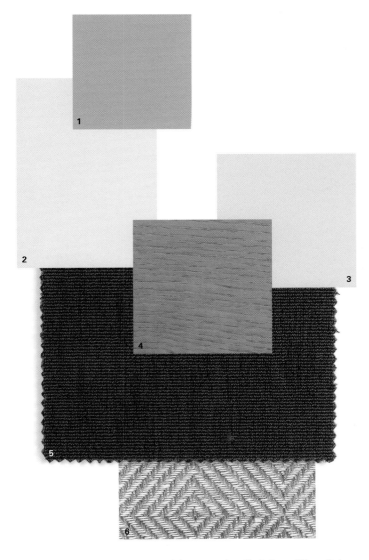

PALETTE 2 Plummy gray mixed with warm brown and purple. 1. Martha Stewart Signature, Monk's Cloth, 8396. 2. Martha Stewart Signature, Grape Cluster, 8350. 3. Groves Bros. Fabrics, Mattias, 1502-GR-S.

PALETTE 3 Cool blue grays accented with yellow. 1. Pratt & Lambert, Sage Gray, POR-2210-000. 2. Pratt & Lambert, Chamois, POR-2108-000. 3. Pratt & Lambert, Carbonite, POR-2202-000. 4. Martha Stewart Signature Fabrics, Chrysanthemum, Robin's Egg, MSH-00010F. 5. Melrose House, Rose Tarlow, Velours Cord, Lichen, 2033/02.

PALETTE 1 Warm grays with a touch of pink. 1. Fine Paints of Europe, the Skylands Colors, Fog, 11. 2. Fine Paints of Europe, the Skylands Colors, Pink Granite, 1. 3. Fine Paints of Europe, the Skylands Colors, Skylands Gray, 31. 4. Gray washed oak. 5. Holly Hunt, Great Plains, Loam, Anthracite, 502/02. 6. Country Swedish, Rye, White/Beige, 208-81.

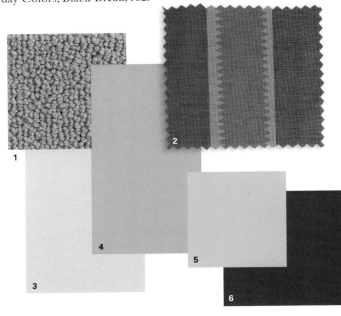

PALETTE 2 Pink plus brown—always works, never too sweet. **1.** Masland, Landscape, Wind Drift, 7218-263. **2.** Bennison, Teeth Stripe, Pink Brown. **3.** Pratt & Lambert, Chamois, POR-2108-000. **4.** Martha Stewart Everyday Colors, Coral Bells, A06. **5.** Martha Stewart Everyday Colors, Old Brick, A11. **6.** Martha Stewart Everyday Colors, Black Bread, F02.

PALETTE 1 Clear, true pinks set off with chartreuse green. **1.** Smith + Noble window blinds, Honey Oak, 272. **2.** Manuel Canovas, Cotton Club, 4275/22. **3.** Pratt & Lambert, Demoiselle, POR-1838-000. **4.** Martha Stewart Everyday Colors, Dill Flower, E28. **5.** Martha Stewart Everyday Colors, Caneware, H09. **6.** Summer Hill, Puff Piqué 1416, Melon, 09. **7.** Martha Stewart Signature Fabrics, Butterflies and Blossoms, Peony, MSH00093F. **8.** Martha Stewart Everyday Colors, Bee Balm Red, A02.

PALETTE 3 Misty pink mixed with a moody neutral for an elegant feel. **1.** Fine Paints of Europe, the Skylands Colors, Pink Granite, 1. **2.** Fine Paints of Europe, the Araucana Colors, Araucana Wheaten, 20. **3.** Clarence House, Damas Alicante, 31808-14.

sources

IRONSTONE

PAGE 14 Special thanks to Mr. and Mrs. Winthrop S. Pike, Kristina P. Hadinger, Karen E. Pike, and Amy P. Sharpless.

PAGE 15 SWEDISH CHAIR, from Treillage, 418 East 75th Street, New York, NY 10021; 212-535-2288. Martha Stewart Everyday Colors PAINT in Ursa Minor (H18), available at Kmart stores; 800-866-0086; also available at Sears stores, 800-972-4687 for locations. Benjamin Moore white oil SEMIGLOSS (235-01, on trim); 800-826-2623 for nearest retailer. Regency square-back BAMBOO CHAIR, $2,310, from Waldo's Design, 223 East 58th Street, New York, NY 10022; 212-308-8688. Egg PRINTS, $30 each from Pageant Books and Prints, P.O. Box 1081, New York, NY 10013-0862; 212-674-5296. FRAMES, from IKEA; 410-931-8940 or 410-931-5400 for East Coast locations and 619-563-4532 or 626-912-4532 for West Coast locations.

PAGE 17 Silk LAMPSHADES from Oriental Lamp Shade Company, 816 Lexington Avenue, New York, NY 10021; 212-832-8190. Beaded FRINGE (TH556), $20 per yd., from Tinsel Trading Company, 47 West 38th Street, New York, NY 10018; 212-730-1030.

PAGE 18 CUP AND TOOTHBRUSH HOLDER (IBA001), $36, from Martha by Mail; 800-950-7130 or www.marthastewart.com.

PAGE 19 Special thanks to Ina Brosseau Marx of the Finishing School, 50 Carnation Avenue, Floral Park, NY 11001, 516-327-4850, and to Pat Niehaus, the Wall Doctor, 765-296-2871 or walldoctor@yahoo.com. CHAIR and TABLE from Country Swedish, 979 Third Avenue, Suite 1409, New York, NY 10022; 212-838-1976. WALLPAPER, from Imperial Home Decor Group; 800-539-5399 for nearest retailer, or www.ihdg.com.

DELFT

PAGE 20 DUTCH DELFT BOWL, c.1760, from A.R. Broomer, 1050 Second Ave., #81, New York, NY 10022; 212-421-9530.

PAGE 23 DRABWARE JUGS, from the Vintage Dining Room at Bergdorf Goodman, 754 Fifth Avenue, New York, NY 10019; 212-753-7300. Chair UPHOLSTERY, from Bennison Fabrics, 232 East 59th Street, Third Floor, New York, NY 10022; 212-223-0373. To the trade only. QUILTING FABRIC on fire screen, from One Stitch at a Time, 17 Church Street, Lambertville, NJ 08530; 609-397-4545. TILES from Antique Articles, P.O. Box 72, North Billerica, MA 10862; 973-663-8083 or www.-antiquearticles.com. Handblown French CRYSTAL HURRICANES with base, from Treillage, 418 East 75th Street, New York, NY 10021; 212-535-2288. Glass LAMP, from David Stypmann, 190 Sixth Avenue, New York, NY 10013; 212-226-5717. Pheasant-pattern English CABINET PLATE, circa 1890, from XYZ Antiques, 40 West 25th Street, New York, NY 10010; 212-337-9821. STILTON KEEPER, circa 1870, from the Vintage Dining Room at Bergdorf Goodman; see above. Woodard Weave RUG, Wethersfield (39) in blue, from Woodard & Greenstein American Antiques, 800-332-7847 or www.-woodardweave.com. Wall PAINT, Martha Stewart Everyday Colors in Morning Glory (C22), available at Kmart stores, 800-866-0086; also available at Sears stores, 800-972-4687 for locations.

PAGE 24 Blue MIRROR (MSL9874) from Bendheim; 800-835-5304 on the East Coast or 888-900-3064 on the West Coast. HIGHBALL GLASS, Plisee TOWELS in Sky Blue, 24-inch chrome-plated TOWEL BAR, mint BATH OIL, sea marine SOAP, SHAVING CREAM and RAZOR, elder-flower cleansing LOTION and SCRUB, bristle BRUSH, Bioceta acrylic COMB, and vet-and-rum AFTERSHAVE, all from Ad Hoc, 136 Wooster Street, New York, NY 10012; 212-982-7703. STERLING-SILVER pieces, all from Sentimento, 306 East 61st Street, New York, NY 10021; 212-750-3111. White Braun alarm CLOCK (0WC001), $14, from Martha by Mail; 800-950-7130 or www.marthastewart.com. White hemstitched SHEETS, PILLOW COVER, and linen DUVET COVER, all from Area, 180 Varick Street, New York, NY 10014; 212-924-7084.

PAGE 26 PILLOW SHAMS, from Utility Canvas, 146 Sullivan Street, New York,

Manuel Canovas, Mascara, 4404/050

NY 10012; 212-673-2203. BEDDING, from Area; 212-924-7084 for locations. Pedestal TABLES, from Evergreen Antiques, 1249 Third Avenue, New York, NY 10021; 212-744-5664. LAMPS, from David Stypmann, see above. LAMPSHADES, from Just Shades, 21 Spring Street, New York, NY 10012; 212-966-2757. Botanical CYANOTYPE, from Andrea Gentl; 212-966-1154. CEILING PAINT (HC-22) and WALL PAINT (HC-44), by Benjamin Moore; 800-826-2623.

PAGE 27 Light-sensitive FABRIC, from Blueprints-Printables; 650-348-2600.

HONEYCOMB

PAGE 31 Special thanks to Paul Robinson. French 1940s oak SIDE CHAIRS, from Rooms & Gardens, 7 Mercer Street, New York, NY 10013; 212-431-1297 or www.-roomsandgardensantique.com. Antique Swedish painted CABINET, from Evergreen Antiques, 1249 Third Avenue, New York, NY 10021; 212-744-5664. Christian Liaigre oak TABLE BASE and chambord limestone TABLETOP, from Holly Hunt, 979 Third Avenue, New York, NY 10022; 212-755-6555. To the trade only. Wall PAINT, (HC-44), by Benjamin Moore; 800-826-2623 for nearest retailer. Vintage white VASES, from the End of History, 548½ Hudson Street, New York, NY 10014; 212-647-7598.

PAGE 32 Special thanks to design director Eric A. Pike and Carl Dellatore of D&F Workroom. PAINT, Limpet (30) on walls, Ladies' Phaeton (15) on trim, and Sweet Woodruff (5) on ceiling, from the Skylands Colors collection (DPE 001C), distributed by Fine Paints of Europe; 800-332-1556. Martha's Fine Paints SWATCH BOOKS from the Skylands Colors collection, $15 from Martha by Mail; 800-950-7130 or www.marthastewart.com.

PAGE 33 Special thanks to Consignmart, 877 Post Road East, Westport, CT 06880; 203-266-0841. Stained IRONSTONE PITCHER with basket-weave motif (third from left); German PORCELAIN PITCHER (fourth from left); and WEDGWOOD PITCHER (sixth from left), all from David Stypmann, 190 Sixth Avenue, New York, NY 10013; 212-226-5717.

PAGE 34 Special thanks to Carl Dellatore of D&F Workroom. 60" natural LINEN, $19.95 per yd., from B&J Fabrics, 263 West 40th Street, New York, NY 10018; 212-354-8150.

PAGE 35 Circa-1810 Directoire DAYBED from Les Pierre Antiques, 369 Bleecker Street, New York, NY 10014; 212-243-7740. 60"-wide gray WOOL with pinstripe, $36.95 per yd., from Rosen & Chadick Fabrics, 246 West 40th Street, New York, NY 10018; 212-869-0142. 54"-wide yellow-and-gray Chechi Como SILK, $36 per yd., from the Silk Trading Co., 1616A 16th Street, San Francisco, CA 94103; 415-282-5574. LINENS, by Area, from Ad Hoc, 136 Wooster Street, New York, NY 10012; 212-982-7703 for local retailers. Antique silver LAMP BASE from Paula Rubenstein, 65 Prince Street, New York, NY 10012; 212-966-8954. BLANKET, from Ad Hoc; see above.

PAGE 36 Pratt & Lambert PAINT in Light Olive (1491); 800-289-7728 for nearest retailer. Fern PRINTS, from Holly Hunt, 979 Third Avenue, New York, NY 10022; 212-755-6555. DESK, from Sentimento Antiques, 306 East 61st Street, New York, NY 10021; 212-750-3111. White CHAIR, WALL LAMP FIXTURE, and CEILING LIGHT FIXTURE, from R. Cacciola Antiques, 993 Post Road East, Westport, CT 06880; 203-222-1002. Dog PRINTS, from Paula Rubenstein, 65 Prince Street, New York, NY 10012; 212-966-8954. SOFA, from Gomez Associates, 504-506 East 74th Street, New York, NY 10021; 212-288-6856. Benjamin Moore PAINT in Huntington Beige (HC-22 on wall and HC-227 on ceiling); 800-826-2623 for nearest retailer. Farmington MIRROR, from Mrs. MacDougall at Hinson & Co., 979 Third Avenue, New York, NY 10022; 212-688-7754. Brown VASE, from Karl Kemp Antiques, 36 East 10th Street, New York, NY 10003; 212-254-1877. CONSOLE, from John Rosselli, 523 East 73rd Street, New York, NY 10021; 212-772-2137.

PAGE 37 Charlotte Perriand OAK TABLE and Jean Prouve CHAIRS from DeLorenzo 1950, 440 Lafayette Street, New York, NY 10003; 212-995-1950.

PAGES 38 & 39 8'-by-10' wool handmade Aubusson AREA RUG, $5,299, from ABC Carpet & Home, 888 Broadway, New York, NY 10003; 212-647-1144. Windsor and Newton PAINTS and ROTTENSTONE, $3.30 per 16 oz., from NY Central Art Supply, 62 Third Avenue, New York, NY 10003; 212-473-7705. 9"-by-12" PAPER PALETTE, $3.45, from Utrecht Art Supplies; 800-223-9132. Butcher's White Diamond PASTE WAX, from Janovic Plaza; 800-772-4381.

LUSTREWARE

PAGE 43 Special thanks to Carl Dellatore of D&F Workroom. Antique DAMASK, from Paula Rubenstein, 65 Prince Street, New York, NY 10012; 212-966-8954. 48" silk-faced SATIN, from B&J Fabrics, 263 West 40th Street, New York, NY 10018; 212-354-8150. SILK TAFFETA, from Rosen & Chadick Fabrics, 246 West 40th Street, New York, NY 10018; 212-869-0142. Late 19th-century LOVE SEAT and early 19th-century European STAND WITH DRAWER, from R. Cacciola Antiques, 993 Post Road East, Westport, CT 06880; 203-222-1002. Turtle-back SCONCES, from Chameleon, 231 Lafayette Street, New York, NY 10012; 212-343-9197.

PAGE 44 Special thanks to Paul Robinson, Jocelyn Worrall, and Birch Coffey. Vintage COFFEE TABLE, zinc hemisphere VASE, and Kiriwood SERVING TRAY, from Aero, 132 Spring Street, New York, NY 10012; 212-966-1500. Bronze rain-drum SIDE TABLE, from Far Eastern Antiques and Arts, 799 Broadway, New York, NY 10003; 212-460-5030. To the trade only. DAYBED LEGS from Vitanza, 728 East 136th Street, 2E, Bronx, NY 10454; 212-685-6830. Woven BOWL, from Be Seated, 66 Greenwich Avenue, New York, NY 10011; 212-924-8444. Paint on walls (HC-68 flat), trim (HC-76 high gloss), and ceiling (1444 flat) by Benjamin Moore; 800-826-2623 for store locations. Bill Blass antiqued-nickel FLOOR LAMP, from Gracious Home, 1220 Third Avenue, New York, NY 10021; 212-517-6300.

PAGE 46 Martha Stewart Everyday Colors PAINT in Mercury Glass (G31) and Thyme Flower (B09), available at Kmart stores, 800-866-0086; also available at Sears stores, 800-972-4687 for locations. Butterfly PRINT, from Gomez Associates, 504-506 East 74th Street, New York, NY 10021; 212-288-6856. Glass LAMP, from R. Cacciola Antiques; see above. CUPS, from Aero; see above. BED LINENS from ABC Carpet & Home, 888 Broadway, New York, NY 10003; 212-473-3000.

PAGE 47 Martha Stewart Everyday Colors PAINT available at Kmart stores, 800-866-0086; also available at Sears stores, 800-972-4687 for locations.

PAGE 48 24" TAPERS, from the Candle Shop, 118 Christopher Street, New York, NY 10036; 888-823-4823. Antique Louis XVI-style SIDE CHAIRS, from Paterae Antiques, 458 Broome Street, New York, NY 10013; 212-941-0880. Drop-leaf TABLE and PETIT

POINT on silk, from Les Pierre Antiques, 369 Bleecker Street, New York, NY 10014; 212-243-7740.

PAGE 49 1820s splatter lustreware MUG, 1880s splatter lustreware PLATE, and circa-1830s creamware TEAPOT, all from Muriel, Chelsea Antiques, 110 West 25th Street, New York, NY 10001; 212-929-0909. CHAIRS, from Les Pierre Antiques, 369 Bleecker Street, New York, NY 10014; 212-243-7740.

MELON

PAGE 53 19th-century French faux-bamboo BED, from Amy Perlin Antiques, 306 East 61st Street, Fourth Floor, New York, NY 10021; 212-593-5756. Basket-weave BLANKET, from Calvin Klein Home; 800-294-7978. Reed BLINDS, from Pier One Imports; 800-245-4595 for store locations. 19th-century French porcelain LAMPS, from Objets Plus, 315 East 62nd Street, Third Floor, New York, NY 10021; 212-832-3386. Antique English BENCH, from Nancy Brous Associates, 1008 Lexington Avenue, New York, NY 10021, 212-772-7515; and 2 Via Parigi, Palm Beach, FL 33480, 561-653-0000. White square Regency CHAIR (6001), $2,310, from Waldo's Designs, 223 East 85th Street, New York, NY 10022; 212-308-8688. Late 19th-century hexagonal BAMBOO TABLE, from Town and Country Antiques; 212-752-1677.

PAGE 54 Special thanks to Carl Dellatore of D&F Workroom. Silk duppioni for LAMPSHADE, from B&J Fabrics, 263 West 40th Street, New York, NY 10018; 212-354-8150. Brown GROSGRAIN RIBBON on lampshade trim, from Hyman Hendler & Sons, 67 West 38th Street, New York, NY 10018; 212-840-8393; $50 minimum purchase. Antique pine farmhouse TABLE, from Evergreen Antiques, 1249 Third Avenue, New York, NY 10021; 212-744-5664. Louis XV 18th-century oak gallery TABLE, from Les Pierre Antiques, 369 Bleecker Street, New York, NY 10021; 212-243-7740.

PAGE 55 Murano-glass MIRROR, from Chrystian Aubusson, 315 East 62nd Street, New York, NY 10021; 212-755-2432. Faux-bamboo tripod TABLE, from Anne-Morris Antiques, 239 East 60th Street, New York, NY 10022; 212-755-3308. 84" Mitchell SOFA in Ginger Mohair, from Todd Hase, 261 Spring Street, New York, NY 10013; 212-334-3568. Two-toned satin velvet toss

Manuel Canovas, Cotton Club, 4275/09

PILLOW, from Calvin Klein Home; see above. Green quilted toss PILLOW, $140, and Nepalese "Cathedral" hall RUG, from ABC Carpet and Home; 888 Broadway, New York, NY 10003; 212-473-3000. Brown silk TAFFETA on pillow (92905-06), from Rogers & Goffigon, 979 Third Avenue, Suite 1718, New York, NY 10012; 212-888-3242. Rook silver-leaf LAMP and botanical print, from Holly Hunt New York, 979 Third Avenue, New York, NY 10022; 212-755-6555. To the trade only. Two-tiered Brighton Pavilion END TABLE, from Nancy Brous Associates; see above. 1940s French faux-bamboo COFFEE TABLE, from Reymer-Jourdan Antiques, 29 East 10th Street, New York, NY 10003; 212-674-4470. Striped slipper CHAIR (440), from Profiles, 200 Lexington Avenue, Twelfth Floor, New York, NY 10012; 212-689-6903. To the trade only. Late 19th-century Thebes FOOTSTOOL, from James II Gallery, 11 East 57th Street, Fourth Floor, New York, NY 10022; 212-355-7040. Abu-quality Derge RUG, from Odegard, Rare and Original Carpets, 200 Lexington Avenue, Suite 1206, New York, NY 10016; 212-545-0069. BAMBOO CHAIR, from Antique Cache, 1050 Second Avenue, Gallery 64, New York, NY 10022; 212-752-0838.

PAGES 56 & 57 Alabaster LAMP BASE, from David Stypmann, 190 Sixth Avenue, New York, NY 10013; 212-226-5717. Antique Marseille COVERLET from Susan Parrish, 390 Bleecker Street, New York, NY 10014; 212-645-5020. Yellow LINEN from B&J Fabrics; see above.

PAGE 59 Chambray BEDDING in apple green, from Pottery Barn Kids; 800-430-7373. Scallop piqué COVERLET, from Peacock Alley; 800-810-0708. RUG, from ABC Carpet & Home; see above. NIGHTSTAND, by Pamela Scurry, from This Little Piggy Wears Cotton, 1327 Madison Avenue, New York, NY 10128; 212-410-7001. STUFFED ANIMALS, from the Enchanted Forest, 85 Mercer Street, New York, NY 10012; 212-925-6677.

SPICE

PAGE 63 Camel Thompson tartan fabric, from Christopher Hyland; 212-688-6121. Kensington tartan FABRIC in burgundy (LCF3565) on top of stool, from Ralph Lauren Home Collection; 800-578-7656.

PAGE 64 Tartan FABRIC on chairs and mirror swag, Princess Mary Muted (4740/1) for Lee Jofa; 800-453-3563. To the trade only. Scandinavian round-back CHAIR, from A.R.C. at Walker's Mill Antiques, 549 Warren Street, Hudson, NY 12534; 518-822-8016.

PAGE 65 Louis XV GAME TABLE, from Les Pierre Antiques, 369 Bleecker Street, New York, NY 10014; 212-243-7740. CARPET, from Beauvais Carpet, 201 East 57th Street, New York, NY 10022; 212-688-2265.

PAGE 66 Silver-plated English WALL SCONCE, from Nancy Brous Associates, 1008 Lexington Avenue, New York, NY 10021, 212-772-7515; and 2 Via Parigi, Palm Beach, FL 33480, 561-653-0000. Antique Hamadan RUG, from ABC Carpet & Home, 888 Broadway, New York, NY 10003; 212-674-1144. Martha Stewart Everyday Colors PAINT in Copper Beech (B02), available at Kmart stores, 800-866-0086; also available at Sears stores, 800-972-4687 for locations. Upholstered CHAIRS, from Lee Industries, P.O. Box 26, Newton, NC 28658; 828-464-8318. RUG, from Darius Rugs, 981 Third Avenue, New York, NY 10022; 212-644-6600. French 1940s iron COFFEE TABLE with glass top, from Amy Perlin Antiques, 306 East 61st Street, Fourth Floor, New York, NY 10021; 212-593-5756. Wooden BLINDS, from Smith & Noble; 800-248-8888. Endicott DRESSING CHEST, from Aero, 132 Spring Street, New York, NY 10012; 212-966-4700. PHOTOGRAPHS (above chest), from J.H. Antiques, 174 Duane Street, New York, NY 10013; 212-965-1443.

PAGE 67 Urn LAMPS in ebonized finish, $1,755 each, from Stephen McKay, 216 West 18th Street, Suite 1004, New York, NY 10011; 212-255-2110. To the trade only. Vintage footed French porcelain VASE, from the End of History, 548½ Hudson Street, New York, NY 10014; 212-647-7598. Brown glass VASE, $90, from June Bug, 433 West 14th Street, New York, NY 10014; 212-206-7676.

PAGE 68 Cherrywood SIDE TABLE and 19th-century cherrywood DAYBED, from Les Pierre Antiques; see above. Sea-coral FABRIC in Teak (6014), $84 per yd., from

sources

Cowtan and Tout, 979 Third Avenue, Suite 1022, New York, NY 10022; 212-647-6900. To the trade only. Antique linen PILLOW-CASE, from Trouvaille Française; 212-737-6015. By appointment only. Queen-size flat and fitted LINEN SHEETS and PILLOW-CASE, from Area, 180 Varick Street, New York, NY 10014; 212-924-7084.

PAGE 69 Black pedestal BASKET, from Be Seated, 66 Greenwich Avenue, New York, NY 10011; 212-924-8444. Faux-bamboo lacquered CHEST, from Aero; see above. 19th-century Empire pewter URN with lid, from Les Pierre Antiques; see above.

PAGE 70 18th-century Directoire cherry BED, from Les Pierre Antiques; see above. Montana FABRIC in mole (910017-02), $89 per yd., from Rogers & Goffigon, 979 Third Avenue, New York, NY 10022; 212-888-3242. To the trade only. Linen FLAT SHEET, fitted FULL SHEET, and Berlin linen standard PILLOW SHAM, all from Area; see above. Antique scalloped-edge monogrammed PILLOW SHAMS and antique home-spun beige WOOL BLAN-KET, both from Trouvaille Française; see above. By appointment only. Rose DINING CHAIR, $1,125, available from English Country Antiques, Snake Hollow Road, Bridgehampton, NY 11932; 631-537-0606. Antique white BEDSIDE TABLE and antique white MIRROR, both from the Rose House, 1703 Montauk Highway, Bridgehampton, NY; P.O. Box 34, Wainscott, NY 11975; 631-537-2802. Marble LAMP from John Rosselli, 523 East 73rd Street, New York, NY 10021; 212-772-2137. To the trade only.

PAGE 71 Plaid FABRIC from Zohra Fabrics, 235 West 40th Street, New York, NY 10018; 212-719-9617. Berlin natural BED SKIRT, available from Area; see above. Aero design white toile LAMP, $520, and oak-and-marble two-tiered antique SIDE TABLE, $800, both available from Aero; see above.

SEA GLASS

PAGE 75 Special thanks to Carl Dellatore of D&F Workroom and Stephen Hutcheson of American Silk Mills. FABRIC on sofa, from Grey Watkins, 979 Third Avenue, New York, NY 10022; 212-755-6700. To the trade only. Striped SILK TAFFETA, from Coconut Company, 131 Greene Street, New York, NY 10012; 212-539-1940. 30"-by-40" picture FRAMES for screen, from Pearl Paint Frame Shop, 56 Lispenard Street,

New York, NY 10013; 212-431-7932 ext. 6966. Vintage PIANO STOOL from David Stypmann, 190 Sixth Avenue, New York, NY 10013; 212-226-5717. Antique CHAIR, from Paterae Antiques, 458 Broome Street, New York, NY 10013; 212-941-0880. Antique CHAIR with green velvet uphol-stery, from Sentimento Antiques, 306 East 61st Street, New York, NY 10021; 212-750-3111. Smyrna RUG, from Beauvais Carpets, 201 East 57th Street, New York, NY 10022; 212-688-2265.

PAGE 76 Special thanks to Carl Dellatore of D&F Workroom. All FLOWERS by Michael George Custom Floral Design, 315 East 57th Street, New York, NY 10022; 212-751-0689. Copper coffee TABLETOP, from Klatt Sheet Metal, 631-722-3515. Livos Atrium sisal RUG, from Redi-Cut Carpets & Rugs, 1620 Post Road East, Westport, CT 06880; 203-256-0414. CHAIRS, from Circa Antiques, 11 Riverside Avenue, Westport, CT 06880; 203-222-8642. UPHOL-STERY by Tony Totilo Custom Upholstery, 203-323-4490. Mirrored TRAY, from the Antiques & Artisans Center, 69 Jefferson Street, Stamford, CT 06902; 203-327-6022. Chinese CONSOLE TABLE, from Li Asiatic Art and Antiques, P.O. Box 188D, Charl-mont, MA 01339; 413-339-5362. TABLE-CLOTH FABRIC, wool bouclé from Home Couture at Ellen Ford, 232 East 59th Street, Fourth Floor, New York, NY 10022; 212-759-4420. To the trade only. PAINT, Buckwheat (HC02), from Martha Stewart Everyday Colors, available at Kmart stores, 800-866-0086; also available at Sears stores, 800-972-4687 for locations.

PAGE 77 RUG, from ABC Carpet & Home, 888 Broadway, New York, NY 10003; 212-473-3000. Circa-1910 silver-plated SCONCES, from Chameleon, 231 Lafayette Street, New York, NY 10012; 212-343-9197. 1920 mahogany drop-leaf TABLE and demilune CONSOLE, from Rose House, 1703 Montauk Highway, Bridgehampton, NY 11932; 631-537-2802. Hong BOWL, $1,750, from Mottahedeh & Co.; 800-242-3050 for local retailer. SILVER on sideboard, from Nathan Horowicz Antiques/Estate Silver Specialists, Gallery 82, 1050 Second Avenue, New York, NY 10022; 212-755-6320. 4'-by-6'8" RUG, from Laura Fisher Antique Quilts & Americana, 1050 Second Avenue, Gallery 84, New York, NY 10022; 212-838-2596.

PAGE 78 & 79 Louvered SHUTTERS, from Kestrel Shutters; 800-494-4321. BUT-

TER DISH, from Dean & DeLuca; 877-826-9246. BLOWN-GLASS CONTAINER, from Evergreen Antiques, 1249 Third Avenue, New York, NY 10021; 212-744-5664. Meat DRAINER, from the Vintage Dining Room at Bergdorf Goodman, 754 Fifth Avenue, New York, NY 10019; 212-753-7300. Ceramic BOTTLE and Cordon Bleu DISH TOWELS, from Dean & DeLuca; see above. Glass TEAPOT with wicker handle, $80, from Nicole Farhi, 10 East 60th Street, New York, NY 10022; 212-223-8811. SHUTTER PAINT, Martha Stewart Everyday Colors in Porch Ceiling Blue (C26), available at Kmart stores, 800-866-0086; also available at Sears stores, 800-972-4687 for locations. FLOOR PAINT (834 and 837), by Benjamin Moore; 800-826-2623.

PAGE 80 Special thanks to architect Leslie Gill, 63 Greene Street, New York, NY 10012, 212-334-8011; contractor Mark Silverstein of Silverstein & Associates Interiors, 434 Broadway, Eighth Floor, New York, NY 10013, 212-925-8584; and Dimension Lumber (for millwork, moldings to order), 517 Stagg Street, Brooklyn, NY 11237, 718-497-1680 or 800-233-6534. Crescent Moon (4) PAINT on moldings in the kitchen, from the Skylands Colors collection, distributed by Fine Paints of Europe; 800-332-1556. PAINT CHIPS for the Skylands Colors collection (DPE001C), from Martha by Mail; 800-950-7130 or www.marthastewart.com. MIRROR from Rose House; see above. Pressed-glass COVERED-BOX SET (LJB002), $44 for set of two, from Martha by Mail; see above. Thassos white marble SINK and FLOOR from Dente Trading Company, 30 Canfield Road, Cedar Grove, NJ 07009; 973-857-4050. SINK LEGS with nickel-plated brass foot from Urban Archaeology, 143 Franklin Street, New York, NY 10013; 212-431-4646. Shower-stall GLASS, from Bendheim; 800-835-5304 on the East Coast or 888-900-3064 on the West Coast.

PAGE 81 Circa-1940 French linen slipper CHAIRS, from Gomez Associates, 504-506 East 74th Street, New York, NY 10021; 212-288-6856. FRAMES, from Skyframe & Art, 96 Spring Street, New York, NY 10012; 212-925-7856. ETCHING INK in raw umber and all additional ART SUPPLIES, from New York Central Art Supply, 62 Third Avenue, New York, NY 10003; 212-473-7705.

PAGE 85 Woodard Weave geometric checkerboard RUG (34L), $14.75 per square ft., from Woodard & Greenstein American Antiques, 506 East 74th Street, New York, NY 10021; 800-332-7847 or www.woodard-weave.com. Linen CHAIR, from Gomez Associates, 504-506 East 74th Street, New York, NY 10021; 212-288-6856. Cashmere THROW and PILLOW, from Ad Hoc, 136 Wooster Street, New York, NY 10012; 212-982-7703.

PAGE 86 Yellow POTTERY, from David Stypmann, 190 Sixth Avenue, New York, NY 10013; 212-226-5717.

PAGE 87 CHEST, from the Rose House, 1703 Montauk Highway, Bridgehampton, NY 11932; 631-537-2802. Chinese RUG, from ABC Carpet & Home; 888 Broadway, New York, NY 10003; 212-473-3000. FRAME, from Sky Frame & Art, 96 Spring Street, Third Floor, New York, NY 10012; 212-925-7856.

PAGE 88 Special thanks to Consignmart, 877 Post Road East, Westport, CT 06880; 203-226-0841. Assorted STUFFED ANI-MALS and CHILDREN'S BOOKS, from the Enchanted Forest, 85 Mercer Street, New York, NY 10012; 212-925-6677. 9'-by-12' Bessarabian CARPET (XIX), $7,560, from Beauvais Carpets, 201 East 57th Street, New York, NY 10022; 212-688-2265. PAINT on chandelier (338), by Benjamin Moore; 888-236-6667 for retailers. CHAN-DELIER BULBS, from Just Bulbs, 936 Broadway, New York, NY 10010; 212-228-7820.

PAGE 90 Yellow coffee MUGS and ivory COMPOTE, from Crate & Barrel; 800-996-9960. TILES and installation, by Yonkers Carpet & Linoleum, 371 South Broadway, Yonkers, NY 10705; 914-963-6006.

Hinson, Pebbles Chenille, Celadon/Cream, HCW63700-GDO

PAGE 95 19th-century French faux-bamboo BED, from Amy Perlin Antiques, 306 East 61st Street, New York, NY 10021; 212-593-5756. Vintage BED LINENS, from ABC Carpet & Home; 888 Broadway, New York, NY 10003; 212-473-3000. Basket-weave BLANKET, from Calvin Klein Home; 877-256-7373. 19th-century French porcelain LAMPS, from Objets Plus, 315 East 62nd Street, Third Floor, New York, NY 10021; 212-832-3386. Antique English BENCH, from Nancy Brous Associates, 1008 Lexington Avenue, New York, NY 10021, 212-772-7515; and 2 Via Parigi, Palm Beach, FL 33480, 561-653-0000. Antique floral hooked RUG and 1920s Le Moyne star QUILT, from Laura Fisher Antique Quilts and Americana, 1050 Second Avenue, Gallery 84, New York, NY 10022; 212-838-2596. 18th-century black lacquer chinoiserie MIRROR, from Guild Antiques II, 1089 Madison Avenue, New York, NY 10028; 212-717-1810. PAINT on walls in Limeburst (1064T), from Janovic Plaza, 215 Seventh Avenue, New York, NY 10011; 212-645-5454.

PAGE 96 Special thanks to Paul Robinson. MATTRESS, available from Dial-A-Mattress; 800-628-8737. Martha Stewart Everyday Colors PAINT in Ursa Minor (H18, undercoat on headboard) and Winter Surf (G23, headboard patina), available at Kmart stores, 800-866-0086; also available at Sears stores, 800-972-4687 for locations. Green piqué Dietrich FABRIC (93104-05), $78 per yd., available from Rogers & Goffigon, 979 Third Avenue, Suite 1718, New York, NY 10022; 212-888-3242. To the trade only. Vintage Marseilles-type COVERLET, available from Trouvaille Française; 212-737-6015. By appointment only. Antique round pedestal TABLE, available from Les Pierre Antiques, 369 Bleecker Street, New York, NY 10014; 212-243-7740. VASE, by Jonathan Adler, 465 Broome Street, NY 10013.

PAGE 97 Special thanks to architect Leslie Gill, 63 Greene Street, New York, NY 10012, 212-334-8011; contractor Mark Silverstein of Silverstein & Associates Interiors, 434 Broadway, Eighth Floor, New York, NY 10013, 212-925-8584; Dimension Lumber (for millwork, moldings to order), 517 Stagg Street, Brooklyn, NY 11237, 718-497-1680 or 800-233-6534; and Scott Sandler (for floor work) of Urban Restoration, 200 Central Park South, Suite 11N, New York, NY 10019, 212-799-0703. Sargeant Trail (29) PAINT on kitchen walls, hallways, living-room walls, kitchen cabinets, and window frames; Crescent Moon (4) PAINT on moldings in the kitchen; all from the Skylands Colors collection. PAINT CHIPS for the Skylands Colors (DPE001C) and the Araucana Colors (DPE001A) from Martha by Mail, www.marthastewart.com. Both collections are distributed by Fine Paints of Europe; 800-332-1556. Custom steel WINDOWS, from Hope's Windows, 84 Hopkins Avenue, Jamestown, NY 14701; 716-665-5124. Light Restoration GLASS in windows, from Bendheim; 800-835-5304 on the East Coast or 888-900-3064 on the West Coast. Bianco Carerra marble COUNTERTOPS by Dente Trading Company, 30 Canfield Road, Cedar Grove, NJ 07009; 973-857-4050. Six-burner RANGE with griddle (VGRC485-6GD), $7,813–$8,211; HOOD (VWH4848), $1,529–1,828; and DISHWASHER (VUD141), $1,695–$1,928; all from Viking Range; 800-356-3803 for nearest location. Two-slice dualit TOASTER (1181569), $219; Francis X-1 ESPRESSO MACHINE (1256650), $499.95; and COFFEE ATTACHMENT, $28; all from Williams-Sonoma; 800-541-2233 for nearest locations. 2-gallon and 4-gallon APOTHECARY JARS (OCA002, OCA003), $48 and $82, from Martha by Mail; see above. DRAWER PULLS from Olde Good Things, 124 West 24th Street, New York, NY 10011; 212-989-8401. NICKEL PLATING on drawer pulls by Empire Metal Finishing, 15-09 129th Street, College Point, NY 11356; 718-358-8100. Martha Stewart Everyday Colors PAINT in Vellum (H22) on trim and in Sundial (E01) on walls, available at Kmart stores, 800-866-0086; also available at Sears stores, 800-972-4687 for locations. Parisian Art Deco mahogany STOOL, from Gomez Associates, 504-506 East 74th Street, Third Floor, New York, NY 10021; 212-288-6856. American 1930s WOOD SHELF with bamboo rail, and antique English MIRROR over mantel, from Nancy Brous Associates; see above. Cast-iron oval fluted PEDESTAL SINK, from Urban Archaeology, 143 Franklin Street, New York, NY 10013; 212-431-4646. Assorted TOWELS, from ABC Carpet & Home; see above. 19th-century handwoven BASKET, from Laura Fisher Antique Quilts & Americana, 1050 Second Avenue, Gallery 84, New York, NY 10022; 212-838-2596. Fine Madagascar striped WALLPAPER, from Inson & Company, 27-35 Jackson Avenue, Long Island City, NY 11101; 718-482-1100. To the trade only.

PAGE 98 Wall PAINT, Sherwood Green (HC-118), from Benjamin Moore; 800-826-2623 for nearest retailer. Short-handled linen TOTE (ELP 001), $98, and waxed cotton UMBRELLA in brown (AMB003), $48, from Martha by Mail; see above. Café curtain eyelet FABRIC, from B&J Fabrics, 263 West 40th Street, New York, NY 10018; 212-354-8150. Antique log cabin hooked RUG, circa 1930, 2'2"-by-4'8", from Laura Fisher; see above. 1940s faux-bamboo bronze FLOOR LAMP, from Amy Perlin Antiques, 306 East 61st Street, New York, NY 10021; 212-593-5756. Special thanks to Dan Mazza of East End Installations and Timothy Tilghman. Chinese ANTIQUES, from Hulsey-Kelter, 521 Warren Street, Hudson, NY 12534; 518-822-1927. Double plant SCONCE (GPS005), $42, from Martha by Mail; see above. LIGHT FIXTURE on hall ceiling, from Brass Light Gallery, 131 South First Street, Milwaukee, WI 53204; 800-243-9595.

PAGE 99 Sargeant Trail (329) PAINT on walls, trim, and wicker furniture, and Ladies' Phaeton (15) on ceiling, from the Skylands Colors collection; see above. "Denton Park" upholstery FABRIC in Larch (802001-02), $133.50 per yd., from Rogers & Goffigon; see above. To the trade only.

PAGE 100 19th-century ETCHING, from Aero; see above. Martha Stewart Everyday Colors PAINT in Hooked Rug Breen semi-gloss (D18), for base color, available at Kmart stores, 800-866-0086; also available at Sears stores, 800-972-4687 for locations. Satin Impervo PAINT (HC118), for combed color, from Benjamin Moore; see above.

PAGE 101 Double-hemstitch percale SHEET SET in white and double-hemstitch percale TAILORED SHAMS, from Garnet Hill; 800-622-6216. PAINT on bed in Guilford Green (HC116), from Benjamin Moore; see above. Quilted satin COVERLET, from ABC Carpet & Home; see above.

DOVE

PAGE 105 Martha Stewart Everyday Colors PAINT in Drop of Blue (B25) and Slate (F07), available at Kmart stores, 800-866-0086; also available at Sears stores, 800-972-4687 for locations. Turkish antique Oushak CARPET, from ABC Carpet & Home, 888 Broadway, New York, NY 10003; 212-473-3000. Dining TABLE and side CHEST, from R. Cacciola Antiques, 993 Post Road East, Westport, CT 06880; 203-222-

Groves Bros. Fabrics, Mattias, 1502-GR-S

1002. CANDLESTICKS, from Karl Kemp Antiques, 34 East 10th Street, New York, NY 10003; 212-254-1877. Candle wall SCONCE, from Waldo's Design, 223 East 58th Street, New York, NY 10022; 212-308-8688.

PAGE 106 Special thanks to Consignmart, 877 Post Road East, Westport, CT 06880; 203-226-0841. Satin RIBBON, from Hyman Hendler & Sons, 67 West 38th Street, New York, NY 10018; 212-840-8393. Minimum purchase $50. ARMCHAIR from Gomez Associates, 504-506 East 74th Street, New York, NY 10021; 212-288-6856. Martha Stewart Everyday Colors PAINT in Sand-castle flat (H08, on wall) and Muslin semigloss (H11, on back panel), available at Kmart stores, 800-866-0086; also available at Sears stores, 800-972-4687 for locations. Pratt & Lambert oil PAINT in Appaloosa (2251, on trim and door); 800-289-7728 for nearest retailer. Console TABLE, $1,950, from Matthew, 422 East 75th Street, New York, NY 10021; 212-439-0999. English gilt MIRROR with double arm sconces and display platform, from Guild Antiques II, 1095 Madison Avenue, New York, NY 10028; 212-472-0830. Meissen PORCELAIN FIGURE of a seated Chinese man with bird in his hand, $4,400, from Alexander's Antiques, 1050 Second Avenue, New York, NY 10022; 212-935-9386.

PAGE 107 Martha Stewart Everyday Colors PAINT in Linen White (H29), available at Kmart stores, 800-866-0086, and Sears stores, 800-972-4687 for locations. PAINT CHIPS for Skylands Colors (DPE001C) from Martha by Mail; 800-950-7130 or www.marthastewart.com. Araucana Color collection, distributed by Fine Paints of Europe; 800-332-1556. INK SKETCHES, from Sentimento Antiques, 306 East 61st Street, New York, NY 10021; 212-750-3111. Pencil SKETCHES, from Alan Moss, 436 Lafayette Street, New York, NY 10003; 212-473-1310.

sources

PAGE 108 Special thanks to Paul Robinson. Martha Stewart Everyday Colors PAINT in Mineral Green (B28, on head-boards and cornice boards), available at Kmart stores, 800-866-0086; also available at Sears stores, 800-972-4687 for locations. Blue linen LINING and green silk EDGING, both from B&J Fabrics, 263 West 40th Street, New York, NY 10018; 212-354-8150. Horizontal striped sheer Shitake FABRIC in Frost (92205-03), available at Rogers & Goffigon, 979 Third Avenue, New York, NY 10022; 212-888-3242. To the trade only. Linen twin DUVET COVERS and SAGE COVERS, from Area; 212-924-7084 for nearest retailer. PILLOW SHAMS, from English Country Antiques, 21 New Town Lane, East Hampton, NY 11937; 631-329-5773. SILK SHAWL from Malatesta, 115 Grand Street, New York, NY 10013; 212-343-9399. Emerald-green Murano GLASS VASE, $600, available from Gardner & Barr, 213 East 60th Street, New York, NY 10022; 212-752-0555. Custom RUGS, available from Elizabeth Eakins Cotton, 5 Taft Street, South Norwalk, CT 06854; 203-831-9347.

PAGE 109 Special thanks to Carl Dellatore of D&F Workroom. Cotton DOTTED SWISS and cotton PIQUE, from B&J Fabrics; see above. Wall PAINT,

Clarence House, Damas Alicante, 31808/14

Revere Pewter (HC-172), from Benjamin Moore; 800-826-2623 for nearest retailer. Chinese SILK on pillow, from Long Island Fabrics, 406 Broadway, New York, NY 10013; 212-925-4488. Gray silk TAFFETA on pillows, from B&J Fabrics; see above. SILK VELVET on cushion in sage, $120 per yd., from the Silk Trading Co., 39 North Moore Street, New York, NY 10013; 212-966-5464. Cashmere THROW in Ivory (0918), $398, from Garnet Hill; 800-622-6216. "Eaton Square" Woodard Weave RUG, from Woodard & Greenstein, 506 East 74th Street, New York, NY 10021; 212-988-2906.

PAGE 110 & 111 Mesh SHEETS and METAL THREADS from Metalliferous, 34 West 46th Street, New York, NY 10036; 888-944-0909. Pillar CANDLES, from the Candle Shop, 118 Christopher Street, New York, NY 10014; 888-823-4823.

CONCH SHELL

PAGE 115 Special thanks to Mecox Gardens, Southampton, NY. Framed WATER-COLORS, from Robert E. Kinnaman and Brian A. Ramaekers, 2466 Main Street, Bridgehampton, NY 11932; 631-537-3838.

PAGE 116 Standing LAMP, from John Rosselli, 523 East 73rd Street, New York, NY 10021; 212-772-2137. To the trade only. Upholstered CHAIR and PILLOW, from George Smith, 75 Spring Street, New York, NY 10012; 212-226-4747. SIDE TABLE, from Les Pierre Antiques, 369 Bleecker Street, New York, NY 10014; 212-243-7740. Ceramic PLAQUE, from Gray Gardens; 631-537-4848. Antique silver BOX, from Nancy Corzine, 979 Third Avenue, Suite 804, New York, NY 10021; 212-758-4240. Nepalese "Brush Sprouts" RUG, from ABC Carpet & Home; 888 Broadway, New York, NY 10003; 212-674-1144. ANDIRONS, from William H. Jackson, 210 East 58th Street, New York, NY 10022; 212-753-9400. Wall SCONCE, from Mrs. MacDougall, at Hinson & Co., 979 Third Avenue, New York, NY 10022; 212-688-7754. Black TABLE, from Gomez Associates, 504-506 East 74th Street, New York, NY 10021; 212-288-6856.

PAGE 117 Special thanks to D&F Workroom. UPHOLSTERY and DRAPERIES by D&F Workroom, 150 West 25th Street, New York, NY 10011; 212-352-0160. Wall PAINT, Monticello Rose (HC-63), from Benjamin Moore; 800-826-2623. Framed ENGRAVING, from David Stypmann, 190 Sixth Avenue, New York, NY 10013; 212-226-5717. Roman-shade FABRIC, Trousseau Sheer, in Tinted, $20 per yd., and cushion FABRIC, Lydia Damask, in Eggshell, $145 per yd., from the Silk Trading Co., 39 North Moore Street, New York, NY 10013; 212-966-5464. English country COFFEE TABLE LEGS (1320P), $7.40 each, from Osborne Wood Products; 800-849-8876. Antique hooked RUG, from Laura Fisher Antique Quilts & Americana, 1050 Second Avenue, Gallery 84, New York, NY 10022; 212-838-2596. Painted caned ARM-CHAIR, from John Rosselli; see above. Fluted VASE by Frances Palmer, available through www.etheringtonfine-art.com or 508-693-9696. Upholstered STOOL, from Gomez Associates; see above. PAINT on outside of cabinet, Martha Stewart Everyday Colors in Sweet Violet (G26), available at Kmart stores, 800-866-0086; also available at Sears stores, 800-972-4687 for locations. PAINT on inside of cabinet, Antique Rose semigloss (2173-40), from Benjamin Moore; 800-826-2623.

PAGE 118 Antique TICKING, from Paula Rubenstein, 65 Prince Street, New York, NY 10012; 212-966-8954. Printed linen FABRICS, $190 per yd., from Bennison Fabrics, Fine Arts Building, 232 East 59th Street, New York, NY 10022; 212-223-0373. Restored vintage rattan FURNITURE, from the American Wing, 2415 Montauk Highway, Bridgehampton, NY 11932; 631-537-3319 or amerwing@optonline.net. Antique marble LAMP, from Rooms & Gardens, 7 Mercer Street, New York, NY 10012; 212-431-1297. TERRE MELANGE EGG; circa-1825 English oak CHAIR; antique Belgian mirrored SCONCES; large English BASKET; bamboo SIDE TABLE; 18th-century Chinese TABLE; circa-1800 inlaid BOX; vintage garden BOOKS; and marble PLATE; all from Mecox Gardens, 257 County Road 39A, Southampton, NY 11968; 631-287-5015.

PAGE 119 Special thanks to Mecox Gardens, Southampton, NY. 1930s Catalina pottery VASE, $350, from Paula Rubenstein; see above.

PAGE 120 Special thanks to Mecox Gardens, Southampton, NY. Taupe Samouri presentation PLATE by Jean Louis Coquet, $140, from Lalique; 800-993-2580 for nearest retailer. Linen NAPKIN, $20, from Takashimaya New York, 693 Fifth Avenue, New York, NY 10022; 800-753-2038. Victorian glass GOBLET; 1880s glass DISH; and 1850s red-wine WINEGLASS, from James II Galleries, 11 East 57th Street, Fourth Floor, New York, NY 10022; 212-355-7040.

PAGE 122 Hispanola FABRIC (1351-05), $108 per yd., from Manuel Canovas, 979 Third Avenue, New York, NY 10022; 212-753-4488. Cranberry CORDING (P1509073), from Clarence House, 211 East 58th Street, New York, NY 10022; 212-752-2890. To the trade only. HEADBOARD, FOOTBOARD, and antique round BEDSIDE TABLE, from the Rural Collection, 117 Perry Street, New York, NY 10014; 212-645-4488. Antique alabaster LAMP, from Paterae Antiques, 458 Broome Street, New York, NY 10013; 212-941-0880. Antique framed floral bouquet PAINTING, from Clary & Company Antiques, 372 Bleecker Street, New York, NY 10014; 212-229-1773. Antique BLANKETS, from Gomez Associates; see above.

PAGE 123 Gustavian reproduction ARMCHAIR, from Les Pierre Antiques; see above. Antique pink-and-white cotton QUILT, available from Laura Fisher Antique Quilts & Americana; see above.

PAGE 124-133 MATERIALS and PAINTS available from the following companies: Martha Stewart Everyday Colors, available at Kmart stores, 800-866-0086; also available at Sears stores, 800-972-4687 for locations. Martha Stewart Signature color palettes in Sherwin-Williams formulations, available exclusively from Sherwin-Williams, 800-4-SHERWIN for store locations, or sherwinwilliams.com. Hinson & Co., 979 Third Avenue, New York, NY 10022; 212-475-4100, fax 212-753-8092. Schumacher; 212-415-3900. Brunschwig & Fils, 797 Third Avenue, Suite 1200, New York, NY 10022; 212-838-7878. Christopher Norman, 979 Third Avenue, 16th Floor, New York, NY 10022; 212-644-4100, fax 212-644-4124. Rogers & Goffigon, 41 Chestnut Street, Greenwich, CT 06830; 203-532-8068, fax 203-532-9514. Smith + Noble; 800-248-8888. The Skylands Colors, available exclusively from Fine Paints of Europe; 800-332-1556. Pollack & Associates, 150 Varick Street, New York, NY 10013; 212-627-7766, fax 212-924-8396. Manuel Canovas, 979 Third Avenue, New York, NY 10022; 212-753-4488. Pratt & Lambert, 800-289-7728 for nearest retailer. The Silk Trading Co., 1616A 16th Street, San Francisco, CA 94103; 415-282-5574. Benjamin Moore; 800-344-0400; www.benjaminmoore.com. The Araucana Colors, created by Martha Stewart Living and Fine Paints of Europe; 800-332-1556. Ralph Lauren Fabrics; 212-688-5538. Clarence House, 211 East 58th Street, New York, NY 10022; 212-752-2890; www.clarencehouse.com. Hines, 979 Third Avenue, Suite 1010, New York, NY 10022; 212-754-5880, fax 212-758-4881. Larsen Carpet/Ruckstuhl, 1480 Ridgeway Street, Union, NJ 07083; 908-686-7203, fax 908-686-7232. Martha Stewart Signature Fabrics available at Calico Corners; 800-213-6366, www.calicocorners.com, and independent retailers and designers. Donghia Textiles, 485 Broadway, New York, NY 10013; 212-925-2777. Holly Hunt, 979 Third Avenue, Suite 605, New York, NY 10022; 212-755-6555, fax 212-755-6578. Country Swedish, 979 Third Avenue, Suite 1409, New York, NY 10022; 212-838-1976, fax 212-838-2372. Groves Bros. Fabrics, 5084 Brush Creek Road, Fort Worth, TX 76119; 817-446-5669, fax 817-446-3612. Summer Hill, 979 Third Avenue, Suite 532, New York, NY 10022; 212-935-6376.

credits

WILLIAM ABRANOWICZ
pages 4, 8, 13, 16, 31, 32, 33 (top), 36, 37, 44, 46 (right), 48, 55 (bottom), 59, 65–71, 88, 96, 99, 105, 106 (bottom), 107, 108, 110, 111, 116, 121, 122

ANTHONY AMOS
pages 38, 39

CHRISTOPHER BAKER
page 76 (bottom)

HARRY BATES
page 123 (bottom right)

FERNANDO BENGOECHEA
pages 34, 43, 109 (left)

HENRY BOURNE
pages 115, 118, 119, 120 (top)

JIM COOPER
page 19

TODD EBERLE
pages 80, 97 (top)

DANA GALLAGHER
page 47

GENTL & HYERS
pages 10, 20, 23, 26, 28, 33 (bottom), 40, 50, 54, 60, 63, 64, 72, 75, 78, 79, 82, 92, 98 (bottom), 102, 112, 120 (bottom)

LISA HUBBARD
pages 35, 56–57, 117 (bottom left)

THIBAULT JEANSON
page 9

CHARLES MARAIA
pages 17, 90, 91

JAMES MERRELL
page 76 (top)

MINH + WASS
pages 98 (top), 109 (right), 117 (top)

MICHAEL MUNDY
pages 18, 58, 86 (top), 89, 101, 117 (bottom right)

VICTORIA PEARSON
page 14

JOSÉ MANUEL PICAYO RIVERA
page 106 (left center)

DAVID PRINCE
pages 25, 45 (top)

JENNY RISHER
pages 12, 22, 30, 42, 52, 62, 74, 84, 94, 104, 114

JASON SCHMIDT
page 77

WILLIAM WALDRON
pages 24 (right), 45 (left), 46 (left)

SIMON WATSON
pages 15, 27, 53, 55 (top), 85, 86 (bottom), 87, 95, 97 (bottom), 106 (top), 123 (all but bottom right)

WENDELL T. WEBBER
page 100

ANNA WILLIAMS
pages 24 (left), 49, 81

FRONT COVER
Clockwise from top left:
**GENTL & HYERS,
WENDELL T. WEBBER,
SIMON WATSON,
FRANK HECKERS**

BACK COVER
Top left: **SIMON WATSON**
Center: **JENNY RISHER**

index

A

Antiquing a chair, 38-39
Atmospheric candles, 110-11

B

Bamboo
  beds, 53, 95
  chairs, 53
  folding screens, 95
Bathrooms
  celadon, 97
  Delft, 24
  dot cutouts in, 18
  sea glass, 80
Bed linens
  bedspreads, 56-57, 68, 88, 95, 96
  coverlets, 115
  duvets, 24, 46, 117
  pillowcases, 35, 46, 88, 96, 123
  pillow shams, 26
  quilts, 35, 45, 56-57, 95
Bedrooms
  celadon, 95, 96
  conch shell, 115, 117, 122, 123
  Delft, 24, 25, 26
  dove, 108, 109
  honeycomb, 35
  jonquil, 88
  lustreware, 45, 46
  melon, 53, 56-57
  polka-dot stencils for, 59
  spice, 63, 68, 70
Beds
  bamboo, 53, 95
  drilled swag headboard for, 101
  hanging canopy for, 71
  headboards for, 35, 101, 108
  hospital, 45
  slipcovering the bedstead, 70
  spool-turned, 26
  upholstered, 96
  wicker-paneled, 46
  See also bed linens; pillows
Beeswax candles, 110-11
Blinds, window, 32, 66
Brick floors, 34
Bureau, yellow-painted, 87

Bureau drawers, combed
  gingham, 100

C

Cabinets
  decorating, 49
  glass-paneled, 33, 79
  kitchen, 79, 97
  medicine, 24
  stereo, 117
Candle project, 110-11
Candles, 47, 48, 55, 106, 108, 109
Canopy bed project, 71
Carpet, 75
Ceilings, 26, 36, 115
Celadon, 92-101
  bathrooms, 97
  bedrooms, 95, 96
  color palette, 94
  examples of, 92, 96
  hallways, 98
  kitchens, 97, 98
  porch, 99
  swatches, 94, 132
  walls, 98
Chairs
  antiquing project for, 38-39
  bamboo, 53
  cross-backed, 31
  dining, 14, 31, 77, 105
  fabric-covered, 33, 53, 63, 64, 76
  rattan, 118
  sun-silhouette, 27
  Victorian, 63
  white painted, 14, 15
  wicker, 45, 99
Chandeliers, 13, 32, 33, 88, 106
Child's room, 59, 88
Children's art, 58, 89
Combed gingham drawers, 100
Conch shell, 112-123
  bedrooms, 115, 117, 122
  cabinets, 117
  ceilings, 115
  color palette, 114
  decorating pieces, 119
  dining areas, 120, 121
  examples of, 112

living rooms, 116
  sitting areas, 118
  swatches, 114, 134
  walls, 115
Curtains, 34, 43, 53, 63, 76, 109

D

Delft, 20-27
  bathrooms, 24
  bedrooms, 24, 25, 26
  color palette, 22
  living rooms, 23
  swatches, 22, 125
  walls, 23
Den, spice colors in, 66
Dining areas
  conch shell, 120, 121
  dove, 105
  honeycomb, 31, 37
  ironstone, 14
  jonquil, 86
  melon, 54
  plaid fabrics in, 64
  sea glass, 77
  spice, 64
Dot cutouts project, 18
Dove, 102-111
  bedrooms, 108, 109
  color palette, 104
  dining areas, 105
  floors, 108
  hallways, 106, 107
  swatches, 104, 133
  walls, 105, 106, 109
Drabware, 32, 33
Drawers, combed gingham, 100
Drawer trays, 49
Drill bits, 18
Drilled swag headboard, 101
Duvets, 24, 46, 117

E

East Hampton house, 33, 56-57

F

Floors
  brick, 34
  designing patterned, 90-91
  dove, 108

geometric, 13, 45
  honeycomb, 31, 32, 34
  melon, 58
  sea glass, 78
  stenciled, 32
Folding screens, 63, 75, 95, 122

G

Gingham drawers, combed, 100
Gingham pillowcase, 123
Glazing wallpaper, 19
Graniteware, 13
Guestrooms, 26, 115

H

Hallways, 36, 66, 98, 106, 107
Headboards, 35, 96, 101, 108
Hidden spaces, decorating, 49
Honeycomb, 28-39
  bedrooms, 35
  ceilings, 36
  color palette, 30
  dining areas, 31, 37
  entryways, 36
  floors, 31, 32, 34
  kitchens, 34
  living rooms, 33
  parlors, 32
  rugs, 36
  swatches, 30, 126
  walls, 36

I

Ironstone, 10-19
  color palette, 12
  dining areas, 13, 14
  examples of, 10
  mantels, 17
  sitting areas, 16
  swatches, 12, 124
  walls, 15

J

Jonquil, 82-91
  bedrooms, 88
  color palette, 84
  dining areas, 86
  examples of, 82
  kitchens, 89, 91

small areas, 85, 86
swatches, 84, 131

K

Kitchens
cabinets in, 79, 97
celadon, 97, 98
honeycomb, 34
jonquil, 89, 91
patterned floor for, 91
sea glass, 78, 79

L

Lampshades, 25, 37, 53, 54
Latticework, 25, 98
Leaf prints project, 81
Living rooms
conch shell, 116
Delft, 23
honeycomb, 33
sea glass, 75
Lustreware, 40-49
bedrooms, 45, 46
color palette, 42
examples of, 40, 43, 47, 121
floors, 45
sitting areas, 43, 44
small areas, 45
swatches, 42, 127
walls, 44, 47, 48

M

Mantels, 17, 47, 55, 86
Marble
countertop, 97
sink, 80
Medicine cabinets, 24
Melon, 50-59
bedrooms, 53, 56-57
color palette, 52
dining areas, 54
sitting areas, 55
staircases, 58
swatches, 52, 128
Mercury glass, 17, 75
Mesh hurricanes, 110-11
Mirrors
above bed, 46, 68

above mantel, 17, 86
above sink, 80, 97
against gray wall, 106
aged, 95
Chippendale-style, 85
gilded, 32
in medicine cabinet, 24
Monogrammed pillowcase, 123
Mudrooms, 98

P

Parlors, 32
Paw Paw, 34
Pillows, 26, 35, 45, 46, 67, 68, 88,
95, 96, 123
Plaid fabrics, 62, 63, 64
Plate collections, 23, 47, 48, 69
Polka-dot stencils, 59
Porches, 99
Pottery collections, 98, 117
Prints, leaf, 81
Projects
antiquing a chair, 38-39
atmospheric candles, 110-11
combed gingham drawers, 100
decorating hidden spaces, 49
designing patterned floor, 90-91
dot cutouts, 18
drilled swag headboard, 101
enhancing pillowcases, 123
glazing wallpaper, 19
hanging a canopy, 71
leaf prints, 81
polka-dot stencils, 59
sun-silhouette chairs, 27

Q

Quilts, 35, 45, 56-57, 95, 123

R

Reflective objects, 17, 43, 76
See also mirrors
Rugs
brown, 115
cool-gray, 108
geometric, 68, 109
hooked, 95
rag-style, 85
sand-colored, 75

sea-grass, 36, 118
sisal, 43, 53

S

Sconces
crystal, 16
etched, 34
gilding in, 116
mirrored, 43
silver-plated, 77
white shades for, 66
Screens, folding, 63, 95, 122
Sea glass, 72-81
bathrooms, 80
color palette, 74
dining areas, 77
examples of, 72
floors, 78
kitchens, 78, 79
living rooms, 75
swatches, 74, 130
Sea-grass rugs, 36, 118
Shades, window, 34, 117, 118
Sisal rugs, 43, 53
Sitting areas
conch shell, 118
ironstone, 16
lustreware, 43, 44
melon, 55
spice, 63, 66, 67
See also living rooms
Small areas
decorating hidden spaces in, 49
jonquil, 85, 86
lustreware, 45
spice, 69
Sofas
brown velvet, 67
damask, 32
silk-tufted, 75
taupe and beige, 16
white upholstered, 43
wood-framed, 31
Spice, 60-71
bedrooms, 63, 68, 70
color palette, 62
dining areas, 64
hallways, 66

sitting areas, 63, 66, 67
swatches, 62, 129
walls, 66
Stainless steel appliances, 97
Staircases, 58
Stencils, polka-dot, 59
Sun-silhouette chairs, 27
Swatches
celadon, 94, 132
conch shell, 114, 134
Delft, 22, 125
dove, 104, 133
honeycomb, 30, 126
ironstone, 12, 124
jonquil, 84, 131
lustreware, 42, 127
melon, 52, 128
sea glass, 74, 130
spice, 62, 129
Swatch Guide, 124-35

T

Table, glass-topped, 65
Table, iron, 63
Table settings, 120, 121
Tartan, 62, 63, 64
Toile de Jouy, 65, 117, 122
Turkey Hill (Westport) house, 32,
34, 99, 121

W

Wallpaper, glazing, 19
Walls
celadon, 98
conch shell, 115
dark, 63, 68, 69
Delft, 23
dove, 105, 106, 109
honeycomb, 36
ironstone, 15
lustreware, 44, 47, 48
paneled, 68
spice, 66
white latticework on, 25
Wicker chairs, 45, 99
Wicker-paneled bed, 46
Window blinds, 32, 66
Window shades, 34, 117, 118

acknowledgments

STYLE DIRECTOR: STEPHEN EARLE

TEXT BY TRISH HALL

EDITOR: ELLEN MORRISSEY

ART DIRECTOR: BARBARA DE WILDE

DESIGN BY MARY JANE CALLISTER

ASSISTANT EDITOR: CHRISTINE MOLLER

COPY EDITORS: SARA TUCKER, MOLLY TULLY

SENIOR DESIGN PRODUCTION ASSOCIATE: DUANE STAPP

DESIGN PRODUCTION ASSOCIATE: MATTHEW LANDFIELD

ASSISTANT ART DIRECTOR: JENNY HOITT

A SPECIAL THANK-YOU TO Ayesha Patel for styling the beautiful still lifes that open every chapter, and to all who generously lent their time, talent, and energy to the creation of this book, among them Kim Agnew, Roger Astudillo, Brian Baytosh, Shelley Berg, Douglas Brenner, Dora Braschi Cardinale, Peter Colen, Amy Conway, Cindy DiPrima, Tara Donne, James Dunlinson, Jamie Fedida, Stephanie Garcia, Amanda Genge, Matthew Gleason, Melañio Gomez, Eric Hutton, Jodi Levine, Jim McKeever, Kerri Mertaugh, Elizabeth Parson, Eric A. Pike, George D. Planding, Lesley Porcelli, Debra Puchalla, Tracey Reavis, Margaret Roach, Nikki Rooker, Scot Schy, Kevin Sharkey, Lauren Podlach Stanich, Gael Towey, Kathryn Van Steenhuyse, Alison Vanek, Lenore Welby, and Bunny Wong. Thanks also to Oxmoor House, Clarkson Potter, AGT. seven, and R.R. Donnelley and Sons. Finally, many thanks to Martha for inspiring us to bring more color into our homes and, ultimately, our lives.